Basking in His Glory

~Vivien Whitewolf Willis

Copyright © 2014,2019 edition Vivien Whitewolf Willis
All rights reserved.

Published in the United States of America by
Jesus, King of Glory Publishing Co.
100 NE 641 rd. Montserrat, Missouri 65336

Editor and Cover Designer: Vivien Willis
Cover Photo: ID 47351925 © Konradbak|, Dreamstime.com

ISBN-10: 0615923925
ISBN-13: 978-0615923925 (Custom)

The Dancer Copyright © 2019 Rick Everitt
Prose used by permission

Scriptures marked (NMB) are taken from One New Man Bible, copyright © 20 by Rev. Wm. J. Morford. Permission given- under 500 words.

(NIVB) denotes: "Scriptures taken from the HOLY BIBLE, NEW INTERNATIONAL VERSION, Copyright @ 1973, 1978, 1984. Permission of Zondervan Bible Publishers."

Scriptures marked (KJV) are taken from the King James Version of the Bible, copyright © 1977,1984,1990, Thomas Nelson Publishers.

Scripture quotations marked TPT are from The Passion Translation Copyright @ 2017,2018 by Broadstreet Publishing Group,LLC, used by permission. All rights reserved. ThePassionTranslation.com.

In the Bible references and in the text of this book,
I will capitalize any pronoun referring to the Lord.
I do this to honor His name!

He will love us forever~

I HAVE NOT CREATED MAN

THAT HE MIGHT BE HELD IN BONDAGE.

I HAVE NOT CREATED MAN

THAT HE MIGHT BE A SLAVE TO THE EVIL

OF THE WORLD.

I HAVE CREATED MAN

THAT HE MIGHT WALK IN MY LIGHT,

AND STAND

IN

MY PRESENCE;

THAT I MIGHT TAKE HIM IN MY ARMS

AND

LOVE HIM FOREVER!

-Vivien Whitewolf Willis

DEDICATION:

To the love of my life and best friend, my husband,

Jerry Willis who passed into the arms of Jesus

January 29,2015.

To my wonderful children, grandchildren,

and great grandchildren!

To my extended families and special friends.

To all my brothers and sisters in Christ Jesus.

CONTENTS

Dedication: vi
Contents: v
Welcome: vii
Acknowledgments: i-9
The Invitation: ii-10
About the Author: 223

Chapter :	Name:	Page:
1	GOD'S GLORY IS HIS LOVE	1
2	TASTE AND SEE	7
3	WHO IS THIS KING JESUS?	13
4	OH, JESUS, OH, JESUS	17
5	I AM HOLY!	23
6	JESUS-OUR PERFECTION	29
7	HIS LOVE GIFT	39
8	A HEART SET AFIRE	45
9	APPREHENDING DIVINE GIFTS	51
10	APPREHENDING BY FAITH	55
11	HIS BOUNTIFUL GRACE	63
12	HIS CROSS-OUR TRANSFORMATION	71
13	CHRIST AND THE CROSS	75
14	THE NEW TESTAMENT	79
15	THE CUP!	85
16	THE SEALED SCROLL	93
17	THE FAN AND THE FIRE	105
18	THE WAY OF HOLINESS	113
19	REVELATION—THE MIND OF CHRIST	125
20	WHAT HAPPENED IN PARADISE?	133
21	A SUITCASE LABELED "FEAR"	143

22	CHOOSE LIFE OR DEATH!	153
23	WE HAVE A NOW GOD	157
24	GOD'S WORKSHOP ON HEALING	165
25	DISCERNING HIS BODY	169
26	FASTING AND REJOICING	175
27	ENTERING INTO HIS GLORY	181
28	THE UNKNOWN LANGUAGE	191
29	ANGELS, ANGELS	201
30	THE SEVEN EYES OF GOD	205
31	THE COMING OF THE SONS OF GOD	213
32	HIS GLORIOUS RETURN	221

ACKNOWLEDGMENTS

MY BELOVED SPIRITUAL BRIDEGROOM, JESUS CHRIST: "...he who is joined to the Lord is one spirit with Him."~ *1 Corinthians 6:17 , NKJV*

JERRY WILLIS: You lit up my life and showed me true love. You supported me in all my ministry and family life. You were my best friend and a spiritual mentor as well. I miss you! I love your book of prophecies: <u>MY TRUMPETS ARE SOUNDING.</u>

MITT JEFFORDS: A very special "Thank You!" goes to my wonderful spiritual mentor, who revealed the Authentic Jesus whom I had loved and worshiped for many years, and changed my life. Thank you Mitt for giving me permission to quote and para-phrase parts of your writings from websites and books. Mitt's book <u>JOURNEY TO THE HEART OF GOD</u> contains some of those writings. I also had the extreme privilege of assisting the publishing of his last two books <u>VOICES I</u> and <u>VOICES II.</u> Mitt resides with his wife Cathy in South Carolina, and his life changing books are available on Amazon and other book stores.

KAREN RANDALL: A very special "Thank You!" to my dear Sister in Christ and confidant. She always encouraged me and tirelessly proofread my manuscript. She is also an author of two books available on Amazon <u>UNWRAPPING THE GIFTS OF GRACE</u> and <u>SHADOW OF THE SON.</u>

OTHERS WHO INSPIRED AND TAUGHT ME: E.W. Kenyon, Smith Wigglesworth, Ruth Heflin, Charles and Frances Hunter, Benny

Hinn, Patricia King, Susan O'marra, Eva Marsee, Andrew Wommack, Joseph Prince, Peter Youngren, Dave Roberson, and many more champions for Jesus.

WELCOME!

Thank you for allowing me to share Christ's love with you! Some of you are already mature in Him. Some may or may not have taken that step forward into His arms! Some of you are hungering and thirsting for more and more revelations of Him as I do daily!

I hope my heavenly encounters with Christ's Holy Spirit will encourage you to Bask in His Glory along with me and worship the One True and Living God!

Let this book lift your spirit and cause it to fly free! Let me hear an "ah-h-h" after you have read it. Let it be like a drink of cold water from a mountain stream on an extremely hot day! Hallelujah!

I feel like the Apostle Paul did when he said: "And I, in weakness and in fear and in much trembling, have come to you, and my message and my preaching, are not in persuasive wise words but in proof of Spirit and Power so that your faith would not be in the wisdom of men but in the Power of God. " ~*1 Cor. 2:3-5, NMB.*

I truly believe you are going to be blessed by Jesus as you begin to read and believe ! The experiences, visions, dreams, and words were not given to me to glorify myself but to encourage others that the Spirit-filled walk with Jesus is marvelous and assessable to us all!

As always, I ask that you if you have any questions

whether the testimonies in this book are true, just pray to the Father in the name of Jesus and also check your Bible. The Word will confirm the truth. In fact, when I have a vision or revelation, I always check on the Word to see if it is verified.

This book is a result of my desire to move deeper into the Heart of God. I have done many things in my life that I recognized were selfish above everything and everyone else in my life. I put Self on the throne of my heart and I have suffered many years of remorse because of doing that ...but then Jesus set me free from all that. I became literally a new person in Him. I wanted to create a book that would lead others to the One who desires to deliver them from all their sins and regrets of their past like He has delivered me.

I also wanted the book to be broken into bite size parts so that busy people could quickly read one chapter at a time.

My new book that will be coming forth later THE GLORIOUS WHORE, will be a journey to even deeper understanding of Genesis, what happened in the Garden, and how it affected Man's whole universe.

THE INVITATION:

Come now; behold Him! Jesus, King of Glory! Come! Touch the hem of His garment. You will be transformed by it. Come closer now! Can you see His arms reaching out to you, beckoning you to come to Him?

Look into His eyes! His eyes are blue like a beautiful mountain stream reflecting the blue of the sky. They say that His blue eyes come from His mother's side, genetically from the house of Judah. Look into them now, and you will see your reflection. All His attention is on you and for you!

He knows you completely. He loves you more than you could ever imagine! He has collected every tear that has dropped from your eyes. He has held you in your darkest hour. He loves to hear your laughter and see your eyes sparkle with joy. He knows if you prefer vanilla or chocolate ice cream.

Jesus was there at your birth. He was the One who created you and brought you forth from your mother's womb. He still remembers touching your tiny hand and whispering, "You are Mine!"

He remembers even earlier than that before the foundation of this earth. He kissed your cheek and hugged you the moment you left heaven for your assignment, "earth." He told you: "No matter what happens, always remember, I love you!"

Then the veil of flesh came between you and heaven And He shed tears over the separation and began pining for your heavenly return. Now, He spends time caring for you by His Holy Spirit.

Jesus and our relationship with Him is what this book is all about. Let me share with you what the Holy Spirit has shown me about the beauty of Jesus. Let Him fill up your senses! Let us bask together in His glory and worship Him! Let us honor Him, King of Kings, Lord of Lords!

"Lift up your heads, o ye gates; And be ye lifted up, ye everlasting door; And the King of Glory shall come in. Who is this King of Glory? The Lord of Hosts, He is the King of Glory, Selah." ~*Psalm 24:9-10, KJV*

BASKING

IN

HIS GLORY

1 GOD'S GLORY IS HIS LOVE!

"As truly as I live, all the earth will be filled with the glory of the Lord." ~*Numbers 14:21, NMB*

After a sound sleep one morning, I awoke and immediately saw a small, open vision. It was a beautiful one: A vibrant blue, blue sky was partially covered with fluffy white clouds. The clouds parted and there written in large gold letters was the following phrase: GOD'S GLORY IS HIS LOVE! Then the image drew back like a camera panning back so you can see more. As it did, I saw the bottom rim of an eye and knew I was looking into the Eye of Heaven!

The Lord spoke and said, "You are the Apple of My Eye."

"Keep me as the apple of your eye; hide me in the shadow of your wings." ~*Psalms. 17:8, NIVB*

Oh, how my heart is thrilled and lifted up as I contemplate the love that our glorious Christ has for each of us! Oh, what a glorious High Priest we have who intercedes for us minute by minute! Does He intercede only for us during our times of trials? Does He intercede only during our times of repentance? No, our Glorious Savior's complete attention is on His children.

Everything He thinks and does is about how to benefit His children and draw them close to Him! He is indeed like a mother hen that gathers her chicks next to her as close as she can get them. She lifts her wings and pulls those chicks under them. Is it just for protection? No! She loves them!

Recently as I was contemplating this analogy about the mother hen, the Lord reminded me of a story I once heard (true or false, I do not know). There had been a wild fire and some men went to inspect the burned remains. While there, they saw a mother fowl burned to death. She lay there, her wings charred and stiff. Then suddenly out from under her lifeless body popped her lively chicks. She had suffered the fire's scorching flames and covered her chicks to save them. I wept. Jesus said to me: "This is how much I love My children!"

Some say that God's Glory is His manifested presence.

Some say that God's Glory is His wisdom.

Some say that God's Glory is His substance.

His Glory is all of these, but it can be all explained in one word: LOVE!

"Let us love one another, for love comes from God. Everyone who loves has been born of God and knows God...because God is love." *~1 John 4:7-8, NIVB*

He is love! He embodies love! He exudes love! Everything He is and does is love. He allows this love to consume His thoughts, words, and action. And who is all this love for? Us!

"And so we know and rely on the love God has for us. God is love. Whoever lives in love lives in God, and God in him." *~1 John 4:16, NIVB*

He Personifies love through His Spirit as the seven-fold Holy Spirit.

He Personifies love through His immortal body as the Son.

He Personifies love through His Spirit Man and personality as the Father.

He is the Lord Jesus Christ! Alpha and Omega, the beginning and the end!

One day my husband and I were at a hospital. My husband's oldest brother was passing. Jerry was comforting his sister-in-law. I did not want to be intrusive so I sat down a little ways from them. Then Jesus entered the room! His beauty was overwhelming! Never before have I seen anyone who was literally *love*! My thoughts were, "No wonder we are so crazy about Him!" Then seconds later, though I knew He was still there, I could no longer see Him. His appearance as *love* in that room still impacts me beyond measure.

The Father, "Who rescued us from the authority of the darkness and transferred us to the kingdom of the Son by His love, in Whom we have the redemption, the forgiveness of sins." ~*Col. 1:13-14, NMB,*

One morning as my husband Jerry and I sat at the kitchen table studying scripture and praising Jesus, I experienced a vision:

Great wings appeared over us and sheltered us-eagles wings! They were not the wings of a Bald Eagle. The feathers on the eagle that I saw were brownish and golden. It was a Golden Eagle. As I looked into His eyes, I was expecting the piercing eyes of an eagle, but instead they were warm, wonderful, beautiful, and loving eyes!

I was reminded of the scripture:

"He that dwells in the secret place of the Most High will abide under the shadow of the Almighty... He will cover you, with His feathers and under His wings you will find refuge. His truth will be your shield and buckler. You will not be afraid of the terror by night, nor of the arrow that flies by day, nor of pestilence that walks in darkness, nor of the destruction that wastes at noonday. A thousand will fall at your side, and ten thousand at your right hand, but it will not come near you! Only with your eyes will you behold, and see the reward of the wicked. Because you have made the Lord, Who is my refuge, The Most High, your habitation: there will no evil befall you, neither will any plague come near your dwelling. For He will give His angels, charge over you, to keep you, in all your ways!" ~*Psalms 91:1, 4-11,NMB*

Hallelujah!

This is the *Great Tidings the angels brought*: That man and God through Jesus Christ could be reconciled. And that man could live and remain under the protection of those loving wings and in His Glory forever!

The more we taste of Him, the more we fill up with His Holy Spirit. The more we love and worship Him, the more we will bask in that Love-Glory relationship. His love and manifold presence are addictive!

Early one morning close to Valentines day, I woke up to a beautiful experience. It was about 5:00 a.m. and I asked the Lord what was on His mind.

He spoke and showed me a vision simultaneously. He said,"My Love is forever and forever blooming!"

At the same time that I heard Him, I saw a row of beautiful white flowers bloom one right after another, after another, into infinity.

Then He said, "Love is the Life blood of all things."

I saw a small round artery with *liquid love* flowing through it.

"I am the vine, ye are the branches."

I saw that artery carry *liquid love* to the tips of the branches and then back through them to the vine roots.

"Love always seeks a receiver." He informed me.

I saw in vision an eagle flying in the sky. "Why create if there is no one to see it, to enjoy it?" He asked.

"Have I not said I have created all things for my pleasure? Well, My greatest pleasure is giving My children pleasure."

"My love is ever flowing and overflowing, always seeking someone who will receive it and return it back to

Me."

"Will you be My Valentine?"

"Yes, Lord!" I answered, a bit surprised by the question. "I will always and forever be your valentine. You are my hearts desire."

2 TASTE AND SEE:

"My children, I want you to taste of the sweetness of this life, not the bitter. For the bitter must come, but woe unto him by whom it comes. For I have not sent My children here to suffer. But to learn at My hand, not at man's hand. But some have chosen to listen to man rather than Me. Bitterness comes from listening to man, and sweetness and peace and joy comes from listening to Me!" ~Revelation given to Jerry Willis

Let us rejoice with Christ and each other as we waltz through the pages of this book. Let us taste of the fruit that God so graciously offers us. God's Glory is substance! It is not just a feeling but an experience of unconditional love, peace, and joy! His Vineyard is never ending and His loving kindness is forever. Anyone who enters into a covenant relationship with Him is mightily blessed: Abraham, Isaac, Jacob, Joseph; the list goes on.

As you will note while reading this book, I am unashamed of being a Biblical name dropper. We are encouraged and strengthened by the people of the Bible who have had a great relationship with the Heavenly Father. When we enter into the New Covenant-love relationship with Jesus Christ, we begin to discover what an awesome

God we have! We become part of the universe which also enters into a love covenant-relationship with Him.

Visions are not to lift us up but are given from God to reveal Himself to us. He wants us to know Him. He does not want us to just comprehend and know about Him. Jesus wants us to be part of His life, to show us all the wondrous things of the universe! He wants us to spend time with Him.

I was immersed in scripture while writing this book. One night while my heart was getting so full of the Word something wondrous sweet was placed in my mouth. It was sweeter than honey and so very tangible. I wondered what it was. Years later while I was speaking at a prayer meeting, the Lord told me that it was manna He had placed in my mouth. Why the Israelite complained I have no idea!

"Oh, taste and see that the Lord is good. Blessed is the man who trusts in Him." ~*Psalms 34:8 NKJV*

Jesus speaking of Himself said, "This is the bread (manna) that came down from heaven, not as your fathers ate the manna and are dead. He who eats this bread will live forever." ~*John 6:58 NKJV*

I love David's songs to the Lord! They are both to Him and about Him. I was just glancing through the Bible the other day and was directed to one of David's experiences in *2 Samuel 22:8*. David was recording a vision given by the Spirit of the Almighty God in these passages. His experience was fantastic:

The earth was shaking!

Smoke was coming out of God's nostrils!

Fire was coming out of God's mouth, kindling coals!

The heavens were bowing as Jesus was coming down.

Darkness was under Christ's feet.

He was riding on a cherub; they were flying on the wind!

Wow! What an awesome God! He is not a cardboard doll we put on a shelf. He does not make a list, writing down all our "bad stuff" so He can check it twice and judge us for it. It is the devil that makes the list and starts checking it continually so he can accuse you and me. No! Our God is exciting! He has a totally creative, positive personality and mind.

Jesus said, "If any man hear my words and believe not, I judge him not; for I did not come to judge the world but to save the world." *~John 12:47, KJV*

One day while worshiping in the Spirit, the Lord blessed me with a mini vision. I saw this beautiful blue colored bird. It was not a small bird but was simple in form, like a dove. It flew toward the sun and then began to roll while flying. Suddenly it became a huge blue flower. It was wondrous to behold. The Lord likes to surprise us, like a lover bringing us a flower.

I often say, "If people only understood what God has prepared for those who love Him *1 Corinthians 2:9*, they would find the closest watering hole, bathtub, pond, or river and jump into it immediately to be baptized!" Also, the Lord said He paid for our sins "once and for all," so there is no need to be baptized more than once!

When we are immersed in Living Water, covered by Christ's blood, and are born of the Spirit, we receive entrance to Paradise. We have a brand new life in Him. We do not have to wait to hear Him say, "Enter in thou good and faithful servant!"~*Matthew 25:23,KJV* Instead we immediately become a child of the Most High God by adoption, a child of the "King of All of Creation." We become joint heirs with Christ.

Before the sealed book was opened by Jesus, the Lamb that was slain, (Revelation 5) we could only be servants like the angels. But after the book was opened, we became adopted children of the Kingdom! For Christ won the Kingdom for us! Therefore, as His sons and daughters, we are all equal in His sight.

"Wherefore thou art no more a servant, but a son; and if a son, than an heir of God through Christ!" ~*Galatians. 3:6, KJV*

Hallelujah! Only the *Lamb is worthy* of our worship!

One day I was worshiping and speaking out loud saying," Come let us rejoice in the Lord God Almighty. Let us come before His throne with dancing and singing to Glorify the Father and His only begotten Son who because of Love has delivered us out of darkness into light. Oh let us come before His gates with praise and thanksgiving For He is Good and His Tender Mercy endures forever! In Him we take refuge." Then out of my mouth came these words.

Sorrow be gone in the name of Jesus!
Discouragement and depression be gone in the name of Jesus!
Be healed in the name of Jesus!

Then the Lord Spoke these words to me,"For I will light in you all a new flame, even inside of you. It will burn out all of the old and create a new song within you. The darkness has passed and a new day is here. So celebrate and love one another as I have loved you. For I Am raising up a new breed of people, a new song, and new and more beautiful way!

There will be people singing and dancing in the streets. The light will break forth everywhere and lighten every corner. Those who have been chained in darkness will be set free...free to love, free to know me!

I am rending (tearing away) the veil of false beliefs and false ideas about Who I Am in the eyes of all people. Some do not like the light that is coming and keeps coming. They will try to hide themselves from it exposing them and their works. But if they would only look and be touched with this light they would find the warmth and power of My love in it! The light is My love, My power is in My love!

Have I not told you that it is the weak that break down the mighty? (At this point I heard a verse of the song, *A Mighty Fortress Is Our God*)

Have I not told you (He is smiling broadly at me now) that I am not a trickle down God, but a God of rivers and floods of living waters for the healing of the nations.

Life will be transformed. A new energy will rise up and the prophecies of My true prophets of recent times will come to pass concerning this energy.

I am building up My army of new creations, for the old has passed away for them. The weak have been made strong. They no longer grope in darkness but they have seen a great light. They have seen Me and discovered My heart of love, of holiness, of purity and My power working in, toward, and for them. And because of this transformation they will seek for others to taste and see that I the Lord am Good, that I am full of mercy and loving kindness! This has always been My plan to bring all My children back to me...the Father Who loves and cherishes each one of you as if you were My only one.

Come! Drink! You who are thirsty! Come to My open Arms, I so desire to wrap My arms about you, to draw you as a mother hen under her wings. Come! You are Mine! I have purchased you with My very Blood, with My very Being! Come! "

3 WHO IS THIS KING JESUS?

Early on a pleasant November morning, I was worshiping and had just gotten into the realm of God's Glory. The Holy Spirit had descended upon me and I knew I was in the very presence of the Lord. I had been feasting on the scriptures and in His presence much of the previous three days.

That particular morning, I was sitting down with my arms raised, worshiping Jesus! Then I felt a heavenly substance begin to pour out upon me like a shower. It ran down my head and unto my shoulders, arms, and body. It was a different texture than water. It was a weighty, silky fluid. It is difficult to describe in words, but it felt luscious and wonderful! Then I saw a bright, circular light appear. It was an awesome experience! The Holy Ghost had plugged me into the Fountain of Living Waters.

When the vision ended, I continued worshiping. After a few minutes, I found myself in a new vision. In it, Jesus took a hold of my hand, and we went up into the air and were weightless! We could do things like water ballerinas can do! We were laughing, flying, and dancing in the air! He twirled me around, released my hand, twirled

Himself around, and then took my hand again.

Next we flew over a beautiful, snow-capped mountain range! We could see for miles. Suddenly we flew over a desert region, and through a large opening in the side of a mountain. We entered a well-lit cavern inside the mountain. The ceiling was open to the bright sunshine. I looked around and saw great treasure chests heaped over with bright golden objects and jewels of exquisite beauty.

Then I noticed the floor of the treasury room was covered with crowns. I immediately recognized them as crowns which we, men and women, have cast down before Jesus' feet to honor Him. However, I noticed they looked tawdry and cheap lying there on the floor next to the real treasures.

It reminded me that what we have to offer the Lord, which is of any value, is not our crowns of earthly titles, honors, positions, or material things. Neither is it our self righteousness or our works, but rather our trust, love, affection, and our companionship! That is what is of value to Him.

"Even everyone who is called by My Name : for I have created him for My Glory (love), whom I have formed and made." *~Isaiah 43:7,* NIVB, insert mine.

I only had a quick look around the cave.

When Jesus had first taken my hand earlier, He was wearing a simple, white linen gown. It had a blue sash and a red sash that was also simple. But what was unusual was where the red and blue sashes crossed each other at His shoulder. The colors blended in an unusual way. They looked fluid, moving back and forth. First more red would appear; then more blue would appear. But it was always a combination of both colors.

After I quickly looked around the treasury room, I turned back to Jesus. I was surprised to find that He was dressed totally different. He was dressed in Kingly robes and a crown. They were absolutely magnificent and majestic! I could not even begin to describe His crown and attire. They were so... I repeat the only words that fit, "magnificent and majestic!" My eyes tear up now just recalling how He looked.

Then into His hands appeared a small, very plain looking book. The book, like the crowns of men on the treasury floor, actually looked out of place in that room with all the glittering treasures. But Jesus, without speaking in words, but rather in thought, told me the simple brown book was dearer to Him than all the treasures in those chests. I do not know why I did not ask Him what the book was. It was about the size of a paperback book, maybe a little larger. I did not really get a good look at it as it was held so lovingly in His hands. But I did know that someday I would know what the book was. Sometime later, I gave a donation to a Christian ministry on line and received the book in the mail. It was brown exactly like I had seen...it was a Bible!

There are two words I repeat a lot when I pray in the Spirit, in an unknown tongue. I repeated them so often that I asked the Lord what they meant. He told me I was addressing Him as, "My King." I loved that, for whether He is the Father, the Son, or the Holy Ghost, Jesus is my king! my truly beloved king!

4 OH JESUS, OH JESUS!

Today as I was listening to some flute music, my spirit was carried away to declare:

"Oh, Jesus, Oh, Jesus! You are our light, our salvation! To none other do we give that honor! You alone walk upon the mountain tops and on the bottom of the seas! Only You, my Lord, can dry our tears and give us wings to fly in the Spirit. Only You, my Lord, Only You!"

"Where but in the hollow of Your Hand do we abide? Whose name do the winds of heaven exalt? Whose name is spoken on the first breath that a baby takes? Oh, my soul delights at the very thought of You, my Lord! In my heart, I see all the hopes and promises of You!"

The humility of our King God is unimaginable! He, Himself (as Jesus-God-incarnate), purposely came to this earth to suffer and die at the hands of us mere mortals. He did it not only for our sins, but for our diseases and physical welfare as well. His love for us is so great; He literally laid His being down and took the fall for us. Nothing was too torturous for Him to suffer in exchange for the freedom of His beloved children!

"Praise the Lord, O my soul, and forget not all His benefits-Who forgives all your sins and heals all your diseases, Who redeems your life from the pit and crowns you with love and compassion, Who satisfies your desires with good things, so that your youth is renewed like the eagle's." ~*Psalms 103: 2-5, NIVB*

Our chains are gone; we've been set free by Jesus! Hallelujah! How can we help leaping about with joy? Is this not Glory?

The Bible story of little Zaccheus is precious! He was chief among the tax collectors and was despised, even as tax collectors are today!

"And he sought to see Jesus and who He was; and could not for the press (of the crowd), because he was little of stature. And he ran before, and climbed up into a sycamore tree to see Him: for He was to pass that way." ~*Luke 19:3-4, KJV*, insert mine.

Just imagine how thrilled beyond measure Zaccheus was when he not only saw Jesus; but Jesus stopped and spoke to him.

"Zaccheus, because you have been zealous for the Lord, you must now get down, for today it is necessary for Me to stay in your house." ~*Luke 19:5, NMB*

Truly, Glory visited Zaccheus' household that day!

"And as He (Jesus) went, they spread their clothes in the way (on the road before Him like a carpet). And when He was come nigh, even now at the descent of the Mount of Olives, the whole multitude of the disciples began to rejoice and praise God with a loud voice for all the mighty works that they had seen; saying:

"Blessed be the King that cometh in the name of the Lord: peace in heaven, and glory in the highest. And some of the Pharisees from among the multitude said unto him, 'Master, rebuke Thy disciples.' And He answered and said unto them, 'I tell you that, if these should hold their peace, the stones would immediately cry out.'" ~*Luke 19:36-40, KJV, inserts mine.*

Hallelujah!

The King of Glory rode through the crowd that day. Today He rides through the paths of our hearts and lives as well! Should we hold our peace, or should we cry out, "HOLY, HOLY, HOLY IS OUR GOD!"?

Jesus asked His disciples, "Whom do men say that I the Son of man am?" ~*Matthew 16:13, KJV*

This was another opportunity to reveal "who He was" to His disciples whom He loved. They answered, "Some say that thou art John the Baptist: some, Elias, and others, Jeremias, or one of the prophets." ~*Matthew 16:14, KJV*

Jesus continued, "But Whom say ye that I Am?"

And Simon Peter answered and said "Thou art the Christ, the Son of the Living God." ~*Matthew 16:15-16, KJV, emphasis mine.*

"If thou shalt confess with thy mouth the Lord Jesus, and shalt believe in thine heart that God hath raised him from the dead, thou shalt be saved!" ~*Romans 10:9, KJV*

The disciples were growing in understanding, but it took Pentecost for some of them to behold "the Glory of God!"

I believe the question, "whom say ye that I am?" of Matthew 16 is best expressed by the prophet who wrote the Epistle of Hebrews. I will only quote two verses from Hebrews, but all of Chapter 1 is wonderful:

God "hath in these last days spoken unto us by His Son, Whom He hath appointed Heir of all things, by Whom also He made the worlds; Who being the brightness of

His Glory. And the express image of His person, and upholding all things by the word of His power, when He had by Himself purged our sins, sat down on the right hand of the Majesty on high" ~*Hebrews 1:2-3, KJV,* emphasis mine.

This last revelation is confirmed by an earlier expression spoken by Jesus in His prayer as recorded in John 17.

"Y'shua said these things and when He lifted up His eyes to heaven He said, 'Father, the time has come: You must now glorify Your Son, so Your Son could give eternal life to everyone that You have given to Him. And this is eternal life, that they would know You, the only true God, and Whom You sent, Y'shua Messiah. I glorified You on the Earth, when I completed the work which You gave Me to do and now You must glorify Me, Father, beside Yourself in the glory which I had beside You before the world was created...so they would see My Glory, which You have given to Me because You loved Me before the foundation of the world.'"~*John 17:1-5,24, NMB.*

My parents and grandparents taught me and my siblings about the love Jesus has for us. They always told us God made everything. I remember as a very young child looking at a piece of tin laying in a nearby yard, looking upward to the sky, and thinking,"I know God made everything, but how did He get that piece of tin down here from heaven?"

What is a mystery to us is not a mystery to God.

"When I was a child, I talked like a child, I thought like a child, I reasoned like a child..." ~*1 Corinthians 13: 11, KJV*

Who is this Jesus? Just looking at a bug, a tree, or a rainbow causes us to see the great creativity of our God. All the intricate systems of each species upon the earth proclaims His majesty! Only a fool says in his heart, "There is no God." ~*Psalms 53:1, NIVB*

Hallelujah, we have a wondrous God!

"He wraps Himself in light as with a garment; He stretches out the heavens like a tent...He makes the clouds his chariot and rides on the wings of wind...He makes springs pour water into the ravines; it flows between the mountains. They give water to all the beasts of the field; the wild donkeys quench their thirst. The birds of the air nest by the waters; they sing among the branches...plants for man to cultivate-bringing forth food from the earth: wine that gladdens the heart of man, oil to make his face shine, and bread that sustains his Heart." ~*Psalms 104: 2-3,10-12,14-15, NIVB*

When our family moved to a German community in Iowa, I attended one of the German churches as a seventh grader. Skillfully handcrafted wood in fancy designs decorated the sanctuary. It was a beautiful place to worship. One night while asleep, I had a dream vision. I saw the choir of the church singing in the choir loft. I say "I saw" because I could not hear them. There was only silence. Suddenly, Jesus appeared in the air above the choir, and a powerful voice spoke through the silence,"This is My Beloved Son, hear Him!"

5 I AM HOLY

"I created My Own Flesh" is a message given to my husband. It is included here as further enlightenment.

"I Am Holy, and I sought to make a covenant with My creation. But they were not holy, so I created My own flesh which was without fault. I made My covenant with Him and He sealed it with His blood. So man is brought back into My presence. For when I look upon man, I see the Holy blood of Him which makes man holy and I Am able to see all My creation with love! So this covenant is holy and it shall stand forever, for none can break this covenant which was sealed by the Blood of the Lamb. Amen!" ~Jerry Willis

"On account of which, when He came into the world He said, 'you did not want sacrifices and offerings, But you did make ready a body for me...'" ~*Hebrews 10:5, NMB*, emphasis mine.

"All this is from God, Who reconciled us to Himself through Christ and gave us the ministry of reconciliation: that God was reconciling the world to Himself in (by means of) Christ."~*2 Corinthians 5:18-19, NIVB*, inserts mine.

Remember all judgment is given to the Son. (John

5:22) The covenant spoken of here is the covenant God made with His Son. Jesus-God-incarnate spoke judgment for all mankind from the cross. Christ's judgment was: "Father, forgive them, for they know not what they do!" ~*Luke 23:34, KJV*

Hallelujah!

Jesus stood in Abraham's place for the "God-Abraham" covenant while Abraham slept. Jesus was the fire and the smoke walking through the arranged sacrificial animals. Jesus is the Flesh of God, Emmanuel, The Spirit of Truth, made in the express image of God, Himself. The Messiah is the same image as the Father's Spirit Man!

"And when the sun was going down, a deep sleep fell upon Abram; and, lo, an horror of great darkness fell upon him...And it came to pass, that, when the sun went down, and it was dark, behold a smoking furnace, and a burning lamp (flaming torch) that passed between those pieces. In the same day the Lord made a covenant with Abram..." ~*Genesis 15: 12,17-18, KJV*, insert by KJV.

"...One like the Son of man...His eyes were as a flame of fire; and His feet like unto fine brass, as if they burned in a furnace..." ~*Revelations 1:13-15, KJV*

We are reconciled to the Father through His Son, Jesus.

Paul says: "Beware lest any man spoil you through philosophy and vain deceit, after the tradition of men, after the rudiments of the world, and not after Christ. For in Him dwelleth all the fulness of the Godhead bodily. And ye are complete in Him, which is the Head of all principality and power." ~*Colossians 2:8-10, KJV,*

Truly we have a great God, whose Glory will be forever and ever!

The Lord told Jerry one time that when we say "In

'the name' of the Father, and of the Son, and of the Holy Ghost" it is singular because there is only one God! Three in One.

Oh, we love Him so much! Yet, He loves us more!

"Jesus saith unto him, 'I Am the way, the truth, and the life: no man cometh unto the Father, but by Me. If ye had known Me, ye should have known My Father also: and from henceforth ye know Him and have seen Him.'" ~*John 14:6-7, KJV*

"Philip saith unto Him, 'Lord, shew us the Father and it sufficeth us.'"Jesus answered him, "Have I been so long time with you, and yet hast thou not known Me, Phillip? He that hath seen Me hath seen the Father; and how sayest thou then, 'Shew us the Father?' Believest thou not that I Am in the Father, and the Father in Me? The words that I speak unto you I speak not of Myself: but the Father that dwelleth in Me, He doeth the works.'" ~*John 14:8-10, KJV*

When I was told there are three persons in the Godhead I was a bit confused! Who am I really praying to, constantly visiting with? I tried to reconcile this! I realize that we are made after the same image as *they are.* There are really three parts of me: My body, My spirit man inside of me, and my soul! My soul is my mind, emotions, and personality. My spirit man can take a spiritual trip in a vision while my soul is receiving the experience through the eyes of my heart. I have heard from those who have seen their spirit man that it looks exactly like their physical self, even the same size. (Jesus gave us the pattern. Pray to the Father in the name of the Son.)

Paul refers to our three parts: "And the very God of peace sanctify you wholly; and I pray God, your whole spirit and soul and body be preserved blameless unto the coming of our Lord Jesus Christ." ~*1Thessalonians 5:23, KJV*.

So I believe God has more than one part yet is one God! As was mentioned earlier in this book, God is the Father, the Son, and the Seven-fold Holy Spirit.

Jesus, "By Whom also He made the worlds; Who being the brightness of His Glory and the Express Image of His Person." *Matthew 1:2-3, KJV.*

All the works of the flesh were nailed to the cross. Jesus Emanuel (God incarnate, dwelling in the flesh) subjugated the flesh to God's Spirit; reconciling the "flesh" to the life of the Heavenly Father. This is evidenced by the fullness of the Godhead existing in Jesus. This was the purpose of opening the sealed book: that all mankind through this reconciliation could have the indwelling of the fullness of God as well. The Resurrection is the changing of our flesh bodies from corruptible to incorruptible, immortal forever!

"For in Christ all the fullness of the Deity lives in bodily form, and you have been given fullness in Christ..." ~Colossians *2:9-10, NIVB.*

Hallelujah!

A brother in Christ once exclaimed that he was so surprised when he saw the Holy Ghost because He looked just like Jesus! My rapid thought response was, "Why was that a shock? They 'is' one God." I really appreciated that brother and his testimony, for it brought confirmation to me!

"How much more, then, will the blood of Christ, Who through the Eternal Spirit (His own pre-existent divine personality)offered Himself (an) unblemished (sacrifice) to God..." *Hebrews 9:14, NIVB,* inserts and capitalization by me.

Early Christians called the Trinity *Three dancing together as one,* or *Three cheek to cheek.* Jesus was symbolically in the "Bosom of the Father."

We need to pray about this and seek the truth. We have an infinite God, and we need not accept that which is thrust on us by traditions and doctrines of men. We should always search for the Divine Truth of God from God and not from any man or woman!

God is too infinite to explain in our finite mind. Only by the Spirit of Truth can we even begin to understand! His thoughts and ways are always far and beyond us! Thank God that He reveals His mysteries to us day by day. Here a precept and there a precept.

"Call unto Me and I will answer thee, and shew thee great and mighty things, which thou knowest not." ~*Jerimiah 33:3, KJV*

One night I spoke to Jesus. (As a footnote I had been pondering and marveling about the scripture, "...looking unto Jesus , the author and finisher of our faith, *Who for the joy that was set before Him endured the cross...*")

"Lord, I am so glad you are with me tonight as I am lonesome! I will not be lonely now for I have all things in you! You have prepared a table before me, I shall not be afraid or sad or lonely. I shall celebrate my Jesus!"

I continued. "Oh you are so beautiful as I approach the door of the tabernacle. You are dressed in wedding whites, adorned with white and clear sparkling jewels decorating the top half . Oh I needed to see you in that and I realize that I am wearing the same white wedding gown I wore January 3, 2013."

The Lord replied. "I Am a righteous God and I call all my children righteous. It is true, I had great joy thinking what I was going to fulfill through the cross and a sinless life. It was not in My nature and is not , nor ever shall be in My nature to sin. I am Righteous. Righteousness is My name!I Am the lowly spirit that surrenders all for the sake of true love. I had looked upon my suffering children. Suffering from the likes of satan! Their deliverance was all planned, even from the beginning."

"Holy and Holiness is My Name. For I am Holy. I have always been Holy and will always be Holy. I Am alive with Holiness. I walk in true Holiness. Holiness sums up all the beauty, the sum of Who I Am! If you walk with me you must put on My righteousness, My holiness, that which I have won for you! And you have, my beloved."

"Lord I see how your love burns for me! Your beauty is beyond compare!How truly you are committed to me as I am to you! There is nothing but beauty and comliness in you!My beautiful Bridegroom King."

The Love of God for *you the reader* is spoken of in the Song of Solomon. The verses express God's heart for you Read them and rejoice!

6 JESUS-OUR PERFECTION

I had planned on painting a picture of Christ as "the Lamb opening the sealed scroll," spoken of in Revelations 5. I was scraping the canvas with a razor blade to smooth off the layers of white gesso, which I had painted on it to prepare the canvas for the painting. While doing so and listening to one of our favorite praise CD's, my heart became sad. I said to the Lord, "I am a very imperfect person, Lord. How can I do this painting of You?"

The Lord answered, "I am a perfect God, and I can make your imperfection perfect through My blood."

"Lord," I decreed out-loud, "You, being a perfect God, can make this imperfect me and this imperfect painting perfect! I believe Your words."

"Not that we are sufficient of ourselves to think anything as of ourselves, but our sufficiency is of God." ~2 *Corinthians 3:5, KJV*

A few hours later, I was reading the book of Matthew to my husband, Jerry. I paused from my reading because the Lord started speaking to me again, saying:

"I love making the imperfect perfect!

I love turning the corrupt into incorruptible!

I love changing death to Life!

I love reaching down into darkness and bringing forth light!"

At that point, I saw Him reach down into a dark mass and pull out a handful of bright light.

"My God turns my darkness into light." *~Psalms 18:28, NIVB*

"I will turn darkness into light before them..." *~Isaiah 42:16, NIVB*

"And God said, Let there be light: And there was light." *~Genesis 1:3, KJV*

"So also is the resurrection of the dead. It is sown in corruption; It is raised in in-corruption. It is sown in dishonor; It is raised in glory; It is sown in weakness; It is raised in power!" *1 Corinthians 15:42-43, KJV*

The scripture in *Matthew 5:38 KJV*, "Be ye therefore perfect, even as your Father which is in heaven is perfect," has been misinterpreted to mean that God expects us to be "perfect" in our performance under the law. At least that is the meaning that I was always taught by church leaders. However, if we look at the scriptures immediately preceding this verse, we will see that it is referring to "love." Other scriptures will underscore this.

For example, *1 John 4:12 KJV* states: "No man hath seen God at any time. If we love one another, God dwelleth in us, and His love is perfected in us."

And who will perfect our love? God who dwells in us!

"Herein is our love made perfect, that we may have boldness in the day of judgment: because as He is, so are we in this world." *~1 John 4:17, KJV*.

The basis of all love is centered in the Heavenly Father. That is the reason for all creation. He wanted us to have a beautiful paradise! God smiled in anticipation and took such care as He planned every detail to bring pleasure to us, His children. There in Eden He meticulously brought forth all that we should ever want or need.

He delighted in creating every flower and the fragrance thereof. He put exotic, colorful birds in the sky, gave them songs to sing, and lush trees for them to perch in. There were beautiful lakes and waterfalls so magnificent as to take a person's breath away just by looking at them. Fish in colorful shapes and sizes inhabited them.

The Lord created a wonder and delight for Adam: a helpmate made from Adam's rib. Adam named her Eve. Marriage was instituted. They were told to "multiply and replenish the earth" ~*Genesis 1:28, KJV*, as were all the wondrous creatures that God created. God delighted in parading all the exquisite animals before Adam and gave Adam the privilege of naming them.

God walked and talked with Adam and Eve. You see, God wanted companionship. The angels were ministering spirits, but He wanted someone made in His Own Image and the Image of His Only Begotten Son so He could fix His great love and affection on them. We, too, spend much of our life looking for companionship. We are, after all, "just like our Daddy!"

The Lord says to us, "Here Am I; choose Me!"

"Blessed is the people that know THE JOYFUL SOUND: they shall walk, O Lord, in the light of Thy countenance. In Thy name shall they rejoice all the day: and in Thy Righteousness shall they be exalted, for Thou art the Glory of their strength: And in Thy favour our horn shall be exalted." ~*Psalms 89:15-17, KJV*.

Unfortunately, an enemy of God and man was there in the Garden of Eden disguised as a serpent. He enticed Adam and Eve with his lies so they would sin and reject the One who created them. After they sinned, he used lies through the spirits of fear, guilt and shame to separate them from the One who truly loved them. The serpent told Adam and Eve the same old thing that he tells us, "You can become gods! You can do your own thing!"

Trying to be perfect by our own strength and self effort is a hangover from that serpent's lie in the garden. It is that prideful lie saying, "Ye shall be as gods, knowing..." ~*Genesis 3:5, KJV*. It is "self-right-ness!"

Some Christian religions today are still legalistic and teach us that in order to please the Lord and have a relationship with Him, we have to constantly work and strive to be perfect by following the Law. Those organizations "have the form of godliness, but deny the power of the Holy Ghost and the gift of Christ's righteousness." ~*2 Tim. 3:5, KJV*

"Christ is become of no effect unto you, whosoever of you are justified by the law; *ye are fallen from grace." ~Galatians *5:4, KJV* (* "...you have given up grace," KJV)

Righteousness is a gift from God. Our right standing with God is based on Christ's righteousness, not on our performance. Becoming righteousness is not a process! We either accept Jesus as our Savior based on His righteousness, or we try to offer up our "dead works." Nothing we can do can improve on the righteousness of Christ that is given to us at our receiving Him. The Father of heaven cannot accept anything less.

The Divine Love expressed through Jesus Christ compels us to be generous and kindhearted. We are His adopted children so we will want to emulate His personality and love. The real process is learning the art of loving from the greatest of teachers, Jesus the Christ!

"Therefore, as God's chosen people, holy and dearly loved, clothe yourselves with compassion, kindness, humility, gentleness and patience." ~*Colossians 3:12, NIVB*

"For sin will not rule you: for you are not under legalism but grace." ~*Romans 6:14, NMB*.

God does not want us to perform for Him like monkeys in a circus. Our relationship with Him is of utmost importance. Our Heavenly Father became incarnate as the Only Begotten Son, not to condemn but to restore all men and women back to Him. He came to change our concept of Him from a wrathful punishing father ("I am going to get you for that!") to a loving restoring Daddy ("You are my adopted sons and daughters; come up here and sit on My Throne with Me!")

"But God, Who is rich in mercy, for His great love wherewith He loved us, Even when we were dead in sins, hath quickened us together with Christ, (by grace ye are saved) And hath raised us up together, and made us sit together in heavenly places in Christ Jesus..." ~*Ephesians 2:4-6, KJV*, insert theirs.

The reason I am approaching this subject is because it is so important. There may be some who, like me, have put so many burdens on themselves and on others by this perfection thing. I was burdened with this fear of failure for a long time. It kept me from loving myself and becoming a whole person.

As a young person, my lack of perfection caused many painful bouts of self-hatred. Again self was the center. When I became angry, the anger many times was directed at myself. I am including this information in the hope that it will help others who may have reacted in this same way. This self-hatred was not caused by others around me, for I had love on every side. I knew God loved me very much. But the devil plants this fear of failure in us early, along with many other fears.

"For God hath not given us the spirit of fear, but of power, and of love, and of a sound mind." ~*2 Timothy 1:7, KJV*.

I told myself that I had to be perfect to please God, but I kept failing. In reality as I look back on my life, it was all about pleasing my pride.The spirits of fear, inadequacy, failure, and inferiority took center stage.I desired to be perfect to avoid being shamed by other people's critical eye and that of my own. The worst result of this mindset is that I expected perfection in others as well.

One Sunday years ago, Jerry and I attended a different congregation than our regular one. I looked around to see who was there that I might know. The Lord spoke to my heart and said, "If you are looking for perfection, you will not find it, for I Am your only perfection!"

I was shocked! In a few words the Lord had painted a picture of me that I will never forget. It was not a picture of His condemnation, but a picture of His loving correction. I did not even realize that the desire and expectation for me and others to be perfect (never erring) was a problem for God and it still existed in me

Recently while pondering this subject, the Holy Spirit told me that when His children try to be perfect they are actually bringing the spirits of defeat, depression, and failure to themselves. When we expect perfection of others, we are bringing the same condemnation and negativity to them as well.

Because of the inheritance of sin from our first parents, who ate the fruit of the tree of the world's wisdom, we too feel ashamed for falling short of perfection. We too hide behind the fig leaves of our mind. We build walls to hide our nakedness and our sinful nature. But God says to us in such love:

"Who told you that you were naked? Who shamed you? Come to Me and I will wipe all the shame and hide your nakedness with My own blood, My own righteousness! Then you need never walk in darkness to hide yourself again!"

"And be renewed in the spirit of your mind; and that ye put on the new man, which after God is created in righteousness and true holiness." ~*Ephesians 4:23-24, KJV.*

Psalms 34:4 KJV says, "I sought the Lord, and He heard me, and He delivered me from all my fears."

"So if the Son sets you free, you will be free indeed." ~*John 8:36, NIVB.*

The Lord just reminded me of the words to a song he gave me years ago:

    Fly like an eagle,

    Soar through the sky!

    Be free! Be free,

    For in God's love we are free!

    And by His blood we are free!

    Free forever more!

"Stand fast therefore in the liberty wherewith Christ hath made us free, and be not entangled again with the yoke of bondage!" ~*Galatians. 5:1, KJV.*

A long time ago, Jesus took away this bondage from me when I asked Him to! He came and removed from my heart the spirits of condemnation, fear, and dread! He will do the same for you if you simply ask Him to. He delights in doing this for His children. And it is so simple for

Him.

The Lord told me, "Faith is a choice!" Christ's faith is already in those who have been baptized by the Holy Spirit. His faith is also a gift. However, its use is not thrust on us. We have a choice to accept His faith to believe and trust in our God. Choose to reach out and activate His Faith!

"I will cry unto God most high; unto God that *performeth all things for me.*" *~Psalms 57:2, KJV,* emphasis mine.

One day the Lord entreated me."Look upon the beauty of the mountains, the trees, the streams. Before I made man these were radiant with My beauty. There is no end to My creations and never shall there ever be.

I created man so that he would enjoy the earth in all My beauty in all My Presence. But man stumbled and fell and now, like you? Have shut down yourself from perceiving me in all My splendor. It is only you yourself who holds you back from beholding Me in full (His full love). For because of My Son's sacrifice all of Me is available to all of you, to you! My child, My bride, My dear one, My darling how long I have longed to show you my kingdom in full! But you hide from me because you are afraid that you would crumble at My presence. But the enemy has planted those seeds and lies in your heart. For I want only to embrace you. I would take you where no one else has ever been. For there is a place in My heart reserved for each one of you, that is only for you and you alone. For that is how I love!"

"Each is special and beautiful in my sight. Rejoice, My daughter, I know all the desires of your heart and they are worthy. However, one thing remains: to be with Me and My full Glory (Love)!"

I see a vision of a myself as a very young child holding a kite. The kite is floating, it is a bright and beautiful day! The Lord speaks to me, "Do you recall these days in your childhood? Flying kites with your family and friends? I was there smiling!"

"I perceive in you a great desire to know me! I will

reveal myself to you as much as you allow me to."

My response was : "Let me see and experience you in all your Glory Love and truthfulness. Break down the walls and the barriers I never knew existed between us. Take me out and take out of me all the dark places. Put your great light and fullness in their place.

In Jesus name, amen.

7 HIS LOVE GIFT

"Why don't we find it easy to forgive ourselves?" I asked the Lord. Father God and I were having our daily morning discussion. You ask a question and the Lord will answer. This journey began after I meditated on a New Testament scripture several months before. ~*Hebrews 12:2*: "Looking unto Jesus, the author and finisher of our faith, *who for the joy that was set before Him endured the cross...*" The first part of the scripture I knew, but the last part *blew my mind.*

In Genesis, Adam and Eve committed high treason and gave the dominion of the earth to Satan. Hell exploded on earth: death, disease, fear, etc. We get the picture. Look around.

The Father and Son had a plan before Paradise for He knew the outcome. Jesus would be our substitute on earth. He already had the kingdom for Himself; however, it would be lonely without His children in it. The Kingdom was not only given to us, it was to be established for us on this earth. We enjoy His favor now.

All this I understood, but Jesus, *who for the joy that was set before Him endured the cross.* He loved us so much He could hardly wait to come and die for us so we could be with Him. The verse thrilled me! The journey *of understanding what He won for us* has been ongoing. Each time the Lord teaches me, His love amazes me.

"Why don't we find it easy to forgive ourselves?" It was a question I wanted the Lord to answer. So many of us needlessly carry such a heavy burden of guilt!

In my mind I looked back on my own shameful activities, my own self-centered activities. I saw how for years I had wept over the sins I had committed. They had caused others shame and pain.

I remember the 1000th time I had confessed *my long list of terrible sins*. The Lord's stern voice surprised me one day. He retorted, *"I have already forgiven you for these sins. In truth, I have completely forgotten them. Stop bringing them up to Me!"*

What a shock. He did not remember them unless I brought them up? He added that *it was like a slap in His face not to accept His forgiveness at my first confession.*

I thought maybe some of my sins were too big to be forgiven that easily; however, I accepted His word. Jesus reminded me of His words in ~*Hebrews 8:12*: "For I will be merciful to their unrighteousness, *and their sins and their lawless deeds I will remember no more."*

What a blessing to unload that heavy burden of guilt. I realized that *we* alone live in our past-our past failure, past mistakes. God does not live there. Jesus lives in us *today*! He is a *now* God! Remember, He told us today's cares are enough. If we live in the past or the future, we miss His Presence (and presents)today.

"Why don't we find it easy to forgive ourselves?" Back to the answer He gave me.

Jesus explained that we think we are still under the law. We expect ourselves to be perfect! When we realize we have done something not perfect or wrong, we want to go back, fix it or pay restitution. Sometimes it is an irrevocable mistake. So we heap guilt on ourselves to punish ourselves."*God forbid, we are not perfect!* "

The mistakes may have been life-changing for someone else, our children, friends. Remorse overwhelms us and eats away at our being. The devil is our accuser. He pushes our guilt button constantly. He tries to destroy our mind, body, and spirit with remorse, guilt, bitterness, and unforgiveness of ourselves and others. This can even be a trauma to our body and cause guilt ridden diseases.

The Lord's voice questioned me. *"Who did I mean when I said on the cross, 'Father, forgive them, for they do not know what they do'?"* ~Luke 23:34

I had always been taught that He meant the Jews and Romans who had crucified Him. So in my mind I concluded that what I had been taught and believed for years was true.

Jesus said, *"When I said 'Father, forgive them, for they do not know what they do'?" I was referring to all mankind! I was asking Father to forgive you!"*

Joy made me weep! He had asked for forgiveness for each of us, right there on the cross! We were each on His Mind! Our names were on His mind. I was reminded of the scriptures that said He knew us before the earth was made.

He continued teaching me.

From past teachings of the Holy Spirit, I knew that He forgave me for my past, present, and future sins. He told me that He was not going to get up on the cross every time I sinned or repented to pay for it! Sometimes you know something, but really do not know completely. This was one of those times. I knew it, yet did not know it!

Jesus instructed me. *"All of your sins were literally paid for on the Cross. When I announced 'It is finished,' I meant the judgment-debt for your sins had been legally settled. So when you do something against Me or others, come humbly before Me and confess and apologize because you love Me. Instead of saying 'Forgive me;' say 'I am sorry, Lord, thank you for forgiving me.'"*

Hallelujah, He has already forgiven us! My sins nailed to the cross had a new meaning! I felt even freer than I had before our discussion. There was a lot to ponder.

The next afternoon He spoke to me again as if no time had passed from our last conversation on this subject. *"This is why the Father and I had so much joy: Because after the cross there would be no condemnation for any of My children who willingly accepted My love and forgiveness."*

I remembered the scripture, *~Romans 8:1* "There is therefore now no condemnation to those who are in Christ Jesus, who do not walk according to the flesh, but according to the Spirit. For the law of the Spirit of life in Christ Jesus has made me free from the law of sin and death."

I expected that to be the end of the discussion about forgiveness. It was not. He proceeded to bring more clarity the following week!

He spoke. *"My forgiveness is My Love Gift to you!"*

I pictured a gift all wrapped up with a pretty bow on top. What a gift! My joy and tears overflowed. What a tenderhearted God we have!

"You must receive it by faith." He continued, *"You must believe I love you so much that I paid the price for this gift-so you would be free from all the guilt, the bondage, and the sins (the darkness of this world) so you could be with Me! So you could fully experience My love for you! Have I not said no greater love can one man have for another than He would lay down His life for Him. I was talking about Myself and My love for you! My disciples did not fully understand. Not until after My death, resurrection, and pentecost (when they were baptized with the Holy Spirit and Fire) did they truly understand My Love, and the Power of My Love. For My Love burns like fire for all of My children."*

What can I say? This idea of forgiveness being a free gift was exciting. I shared this revelation with my friend. While I was telling her, the Lord interjected another thought. *Not only is it a love gift given to us, but when we forgive others we are giving them a love gift as well!*

This was a subtle reminder of another revelation that Jesus expounded to me about forgiveness a long time ago. I was whining and complaining about someone who had done something that I thought was terribly unfair to me. Was this the first time I had complained about this? No.

The Lord after hearing me go on complaining for a while asked me. "Do you want to pay for what she did to you?"

I was shocked. That had never entered my mind that whatever I was accusing her of I would receive the same if I did not forgive her. Then the scripture which I realized I had not fully understood came to my mind.

"Judge not, and you shall not be judged. Condemn not, and you will not be condemned. Forgive, and you will be forgiven."~*Luke 6:37 NKJV*

"Show mercy and compassion for others, just as your heavenly Father overflows with mercy and compassion for all." Jesus said,"Forsake the habit of criticizing and judging others...Don't look at others and pronounce them guilty, and you will not experience guilty accusations yourself. Forgive over and over and you will be forgiven over and over. ~ *Luke 6:36, 37, TPT*

"Tolerate the weaknesses of those in the family of faith, forgiving one another in the same way you have been graciously forgiven by Jesus Christ. If you find fault with someone, release *this same gift of forgiveness to them.* For love is supreme and must flow through each of these virtues. Love becomes the mark of true maturity." ~*Colossians 3:13,14 TPT*

Forgiveness is a choice! Need I say more? We are commanded to forgive others so that we can accept God's gift of forgiveness.Before we lay a Gift of praise, of dance, of thanksgiving on His alter we must first offer a love gift of forgiveness for all those who have offended us! I have been given *many love gifts of forgiveness* from many others these past years. For those who have given them to me, I say, "Thank you!"

8 A HEART SET AFIRE!

"By Your Grace my heart is set on fire!" (Interpretation of tongues that was given to me.)

November 24 was a very special day! Grace and glory were subjects I chose for a three day Bible study. I had been taking the sacrament of communion with the Lord and praying in the spirit daily, along with studying. This was no intellectual journey for me. This study became a happening. It was so exciting and alive! My spiritual eyes were seeing pieces of truth come together—altogether as a whole, living organism. It was amazing to me. What I was learning was of substance, rather than mere words. It invaded my heart like a flood; the Lord downloaded the most wonderful spiritual feast during that time, and I was fed meat from heaven. It was so beautiful, and Christ indeed became more wonderful to me than ever!

"Howbeit when He, the Spirit of Truth is come, He will guide you into all truth." ~*John 16:13, KJV*

Early that morning I was walking around our kitchen-hearth room. My hands were raised in surrender and honor to the Lord. I began speaking out-loud. (I want to mention here, what an understanding and marvelous husband I had! He was there to hear the whole dissertation and added his support.) I spoke in my prayer language and then made the following statements: "How wonderful the Lord is! He fulfilled the Law; we Christians are living under unmerited favor and grace, and when we were under the Law we were under death!" Then I noted out-loud: "When we are under grace, we are into life!"

I was speaking about grace quite profusely! Then I stopped because the Lord interrupted and finished my sentence. I was saying, "It is when we accept grace..." He filled in the ending of the sentence with, "that you can go on to Eternal Perfection!" He spoke clearly and distinctly to me!

I was thrilled. I repeated His words loudly! "It is when we accept grace that we can go on to Eternal Perfection!"

Hallelujah!

That was not how I was going to end the sentence! I had not even thought of that particular scripture for years. *~Hebrews 6:1* But it clearly made sense to me. In order to go on to Eternal Perfection, we must first accept that we are under God's grace and perfection and not our own! Jerry and I were so excited to get that revelation!

"There is therefore now no condemnation to them which are in Christ Jesus, who walk not after the flesh, but after the Spirit. For the law of the Spirit of life in Christ Jesus hath made me free from the law of sin and death." *~Romans 8:1-2, KJV*

The Old Covenant is the law of condemnation and death.

The New Covenant through Jesus Christ is restoration. His judgment is not punishment, but rather the restoring of everything to the state it should be through His gift of forgiveness! The Covenant of Grace changes the corruptible into incorruptible. The dead spirit, mind, and body are resurrected by Him Who is the Resurrection and Who is our perfection!

A favorite scripture that I will probably refer to more than once is this one:"For they being ignorant of God's righteousness, and going about to establish their own righteousness, have not submitted themselves unto the righteousness of God. For Christ is the end of the law for righteousness to every one that believeth." ~*Romans 10; 3-4, KJV*

We must be humble in our hearts to accept Christ's righteousness as our righteousness. Humility is accepting the truth that "through all our human effort, we can never accomplish perfection." That is why a perfect God had to come and make a trade: our filthy rags exchanged for His Royal Robe of righteousness, goodness, and light!

"He that speaketh of himself seeketh his own glory: but he that seeketh His Glory that sent him, the same is true, and no unrighteousness is in him." ~*John 7:18, KJV*

Some seek right standing with the Heavenly Father through another way, rather than accepting Jesus as their righteousness. They try to be righteous and perfect through their own effort, performance, and works of the law. They may even seek truth through the occult or mediums. As the result of all this thinking, they arrive at the tomb of their own self-righteousness.

They, "whited sepulchers... indeed appear beautiful outward, but are full of dead men's bones and of all uncleanness." ~*Matthew 23:27, KJV*

They will find nothing in that tomb but dead works and the tablets of an already fulfilled law rolled away, just like the stone that covered the opening of Jesus' tomb. They may weep, seeing that all their good efforts and works are for nothing. They may see and feel the emptiness as they touch the cold stone slab of their heart where Jesus once lived. They may see the end of themselves in that lonely place.

That is when Jesus steps into view! With His arms opened wide, He says, "Come; come unto Me! I Am all you need. I Am your perfection and your righteousness. Come; come to Me!"

"Then they cried to the Lord in their trouble, and He saved them from their distress. He sent forth His word and healed them; He rescued them from the grave (tomb). Let them give thanks to the Lord for His unfailing love and His wonderful deeds for men. Let them sacrifice thank offerings and tell of His works with songs of joy." ~*Psalms*

107:19-22, NIVB, insert mine

"For Christ did not enter a man-made sanctuary that was only a copy of the true one; He entered heaven itself, now to appear for us in the presence of God." *~Hebrews 9:24-25, NIVB.*

The Lord told me that the gifts of righteousness (perfection) and grace are received by faith not works!

"This righteousness from God comes through faith in Jesus Christ to all who believe. There is no difference for all have sinned and fall short of the glory of God, and are justified freely by His grace through the redemption that came by Christ Jesus." *~Romans 3:22-24, NIVB*

That same November 24th, I had a beautiful evening as well. I decided to relax sitting up in bed awhile. I was not really thinking about much of anything. Then I had this unexpected vision: Before my eyes appeared a vision of a marvelous looking chest. At least it appeared to be a chest. It was made of a very unique and fine craftsmanship of gold-like metal work. Beautiful ornate designs covered its exterior. It was approximately 10 inches wide x 12 inches long, and approximately 7 inches thick.

On one corner was a button about 1½" -2" round. It also looked like gold. The button was the only simple design on the chest. Yet it beautifully set off the other ornate part. I have seen that same simple round design used for pull-back curtains.) The button seemed to be attached to the top of a pin.

Suddenly, something that looked like very thin drawers started opening up, one after another! I could hear them open, making a swishing sound. The drawers were connected by the one button-pin in the corner.

The Lord then spoke to me and said what looked like a chest was really a book. He added that my vision was to confirm that He had given me a key, His Holy Spirit of Truth, to open up the scriptures to my understanding. I was so grateful to the Lord and praised Him for such a lovely blessing. I will never forget the beauty of it, nor the experience!

Then my spirit was drawn to the scripture, "And they said one to another, 'Did not our heart burn within us, while He talked with us by the way, and while He opened to us the scriptures?'" ~*Luke 24:32, KJV*.

9 APPREHENDING THE DIVINE GIFTS

"Blessed be the God and Father of our Lord Jesus Christ, who hath (has already) blessed us with All spiritual blessings in heavenly places in Christ." ~*Ephesians 1:3, KJV*, insert mine.

"What eye did not see and ear did not hear and did not go up upon the heart of man, what God (has already) prepared for those who love Him." ~*1 Corinthians 2:9, NMB*, insert mine.

For years I accepted man's false precept that the things "God prepared for those who love Him" are a mystery and are prepared for our afterlife, after we die! The following verse, however, shows us something else:

"But God has (already) revealed them to us through the Spirit: for the Spirit searches all things, even the deep things of God." ~*1 Corinthians 2:10, NMB,* insert mine.

Hallelujah!

Here the scripture is saying that the wonderful things God has prepared for you and me are being revealed to us by the Holy Spirit now! How wonderful! We can be blessed with all spiritual blessings in heavenly places in Christ in this life! Isn't that exciting? We don't have to wait until we die to be blessed with God's divine gifts. The heavens are already open for us to access.

I got even more excited when I read from the beginning of the same scripture. Paul tells us who he was directing this beautiful promise to:

"But we are speaking wisdom (God's wisdom) among those ready to apprehend divine things."~1*Corinthians 2:6, NMB*, insert mine

I literally leaped with joy when I read those words: "...those ready to apprehend divine things!" The Holy Ghost has revealed a precious mystery! God's miraculous preparations are already available, but we have to apprehend them. In other words, we have to reach out to receive that which He already has done for us. He is a gentleman, so He will not force us to partake of Him.

Paul did not say that he was speaking to those who "comprehend" the divine things, but those who "apprehend" the Divine!

We cannot receive spiritual things by our intellect (carnal mind).

"But the natural man receiveth not the things of the Spirit of God: for they are foolishness unto him; neither can he know them, because they are spiritually discerned."~*1 Corinthians 2:14, KJV*.

The story of Jacob wrestling with the angel of God illustrates what it meant to apprehend the blessing before the New Covenant! Jacob would not let the angel loose until the angel gave him a promise. But unlike Jacob, we only have to reach out, believe, and receive. Jesus has already finished His work.

Let's look at the woman who apprehended Christ's goodness when she touched the hem of His garment for a blessing. She did not say, "Oh, if only I comprehend the hem of His garment when He walks by, I will be healed!" No! She said to herself, "If I just touch (apprehend) the hem of His garment I will be healed!"

Ruth laid at the foot of Boaz and apprehended her blessing! Today, through the New Covenant, we can apprehend our blessing by lying at the foot of the cross and lying at the feet of Jesus' victorious finished work. Then He lifts us up into heavenly places to rest with Him!

Just as Boaz paid the price for Ruth, Jesus has paid the price for our ransom. And just as Boaz became a husband to Ruth, Jesus becomes our Bridegroom King!

I was seeking to apprehend the gift of Wisdom one week. I had people pray over me at church one Sunday to receive it. On the way home from church, this is what the Lord said, "You have been asking for the gift of wisdom. Wisdom is yours already, it always has been. I Am your wisdom, listen to Me and Me only. That is wisdom. I Am your truth, your encouragement, your enlightenment. I Am your fountain of living water. Your fountain of youth, drink from Me and you will live. I fill you full of living water so you can carry it and share it with others. I also do it for your health and for your good."

One day in a vision, the Lord showed me the most beautiful banquet table I have ever seen. It was loaded with beautifully colored fruits of every kind. I wondered how the table could withstand the weight of all the fruit!

God said, "I have set this table before you. The fruits represent the gifts of the Holy Spirit. All you have to do is reach out and you can have any gift you desire, and as many as you want."

Notice, please, God did not say: "Look at all that beautiful fruit. I want you to 'comprehend' what this vision is about. You must share the symbolism of it with others! They will be thrilled with the fact that you had a vision."

No!
No!
No!

He told me that I, and all who love and believe in Him, can reach out and receive those gifts! God does not want us to mentally/intellectually understand His goodness and His love! He wants us to apprehend the blessings and hang unto His righteous robe by faith, so we too might be healed.

What a tragedy to come to your wedding day and think,"I am so happy to comprehend how wonderful it will be to marry my one true love. Too bad I can only comprehend it and never enter into it!"

10 APPREHENDING BY FAITH

The earlier question of the preceding chapter remains: *Are we willing to be satisfied with a comprehensive report on our relationship with Jesus, or do we want to "apprehend" and deepen our relationship?*

The next question is: How do we "apprehend" Christ's glorious plan and gifts for us? The key of "apprehending" is not our doing works to earn it. It is faith! I am talking about trusting less in self and more in Jesus Christ and His love. I am speaking about making a conscious determined choice to trust Jesus to be the best answer to any problem.

Choose faith instead of figuring it out on your own. God's wisdom and counseling on any subject is freely given. The greater the petition to Him, the more He enjoys it! We have a Mighty God as a Father, choose to depend on Him.

"For therein is the righteousness of God revealed from faith to faith: as it is written, *the just shall live by faith.*" ~*Romans 1:17, KJV,* emphasis theirs

Believe!Only believe on Jesus! Nothing is impossible! Believe and you will receive! Trust in Jesus and He will lead you on the path of your destiny. No one knows it better than He! Nor loves you more than He does! He has a perfect plan for you!

"For I know the plans I have for you," declares the

Lord, "plans to prosper you and not to harm you, plans to give you hope and a future. Then you will call on me and come and pray to me, and I will listen to you." ~*Jeremiah. 29: 11 ,12, NIVB*

If only Adam and Eve had listened to the Great I Am! They were enticed by the lusts of their eyes and the pride of their heart. They turned from God. They did not choose to believe or trust in God's love and destiny for them. They listened instead to the words of the evil one. Later, I am sure, when they saw their dear son Able lying dead, they wept bitterly and said: "Oh, I wish we had listened to God's voice!"

The Lord was teaching my husband Jerry one day about the scripture, "Seek and you will find, knock..." ~*Matthew 7:7, KJV* Most of us are familiar with it! The Lord said sometimes people will knock and knock at the door and He opens it for them, but they will not walk through. They just continue knocking in the same manner as if the door was still closed. They do not exercise their faith in God's desire to bless them with open doors!

I have also heard about how people have prayed and prayed to have new body parts and an angel brings it. The same angel is there to replace it for the damaged part, but the person does not receive (apprehend) the blessing. The angel takes the part back to heaven to the storehouse of body parts, disappointed. Our God is disappointed too. For He has so much joy when we have joy and He loves His children and wants to bless them in every way.

The book of Judges of the Old Testament relates how the Lord would bless His children. They would be happy and prosper for a while then later would turn to other gods and worship them. God would let them choose their sins and false gods. They would be left to fight their battles on their own. Their enemies would win and take them captive. They would repent and come back to Him. His people would cry out to Him to deliver them. He would raise up a judge, prophet, or prophetess to deliver them. They would have peace again until another generation would repeat the process. "My arm is stretched out still!" was repeated over and over again as He extended them His Mercy Seat. We have an awesome God!

Even though we believe in Jesus and His power to heal, sometimes we do not believe He will do it for us. Maybe we think, " We are just not perfect enough for Him to bless us," or "Oh, I am so unworthy." Sometimes we believe we have to earn our healing through works. Oh, how the heavens weep when we think in this prideful way! We need to focus on Jesus and His wonderful love for us and say instead, "But My God shall supply all your need according to His riches in Glory by Christ Jesus." ~*Philippians 4:19, KJV*.

If we do not know that God loves us, wants to heal us, and open doors of adventures for us, we do not know His righteousness! We do not really know Him!

Recently, I looked at one area of my life where I was still trying to earn or figure out how to manage our finances. I saw the result of my unbelief! We did not have an abundance overflowing, so I knew that we had not submitted to His grace and His righteousness in this area. Maybe an angel has stood outside our door with a financial windfall and we stood in the way by our unbelief.

"Many are the afflictions of the righteous, but the LORD delivereth him out of them all." ~*Psalms 34:19, KJV*

As I was writing this book, I realized that I needed to correct this by faith. I literally told God that I was going to totally trust Him with our finances. That very day He showed me the truth that had totally escaped me earlier! The truth often does that, especially simple truth. He showed me that faith is a choice, not an "I have to have" faith.

This changed my whole attitude! "Hey, I can do this! I can choose to trust in Christ! I can choose to receive. "

One time while ministering to the sick, the Lord said,"Healing the sick is easy!" Jerry and I were shocked by that declaration. At that time I was trying to increase my faith. Now I realize that I cannot enlarge my own faith! It is Christ's faith I need to choose to receive. In fact at that time He told me,"Don't focus on your faith. Focus on My Power to heal."

"Then said they unto him, 'What shall we do, that we might work the works of God.' Jesus answered and said unto them 'This is the work of God, that ye believe on Him whom He hath sent!'" ~*John 6:28-29, KJV.*

We are often pounded by the concept that "faith without works is dead"! Whose works are they? Whose works are we talking about?

"Believest thou not that I Am in the Father, and the Father in Me? The words that I speak unto you, I speak not Myself: but the Father that dwelleth in Me, He doeth the works." ~*John 14:10, KJV*

Mitt Jeffords was so excited when he read *Psalms 57:2*, "I will cry unto God Most High. Unto God that *performs all things* for me."

We need to acknowledge that Jesus' work is finished. Every provision has already been made for our lives. If we are born-again all our sins and liabilities have been paid for! Our acts of kindness is an outgrowth of that love that God has first shown us. We need to share His love with others so they too might believe in Him.

"That ye believe on Him whom He hath sent." ~*John 6:29, KJV*

"Lord, Thou wilt ordain peace for us: for Thou also hast wrought all our works in us." ~*Isaiah 26:12, KJV.*

"For it is God which worketh in you both to will and to do of His good pleasure." ~*Philip. 2:13, KJV.*

Faith does come from hearing as well. We receive faith by hearing spirit-filled pastoral messages. Even when we read the scriptures out-loud, faith is increased by our hearing His Words. The revelations we receive personally from the Holy Spirit (Rhema) are far superior than man's words.

"For Isaiah says, 'Lord, who has believed our message?' Consequently, faith come from hearing the message, and message is heard through the word of Christ!" ~*Romans 10:16- 17, NIVB*

One time I was listening to one of my favorite preachers. He was teaching on the 5th chapter of Luke. He was presenting a wonderful lesson on it. Nevertheless, while

I was listening, the Lord opened my eyes to see a different revelation of that story that has been retold over and over. Jesus loves to feed us Hidden Manna from the scriptures. This was the revelation I received:

Jesus entered into one of the ships at Lake Gennesaret. It was Simon's boat and Jesus asked him to move it out away from the shore. Jesus wanted to teach the people without being over whelmed by the crowd. Simon responded immediately to Jesus. When Jesus finished speaking to the multitude He turned to Simon and said:

"Launch out into the deep, and let down your nets for a draught (a catch)." ~*Luke 5:4, KJV,* insert mine.

He was saying to Simon and is saying to us today, "Launch out into the deep! Get out of your comfort zone! Come with Me! Trust Me!"

Oh, the wonders and the adventures we experience when we get out deeper into that Water of Life with Jesus!

Simon answered Him, "Master, we have toiled all the night, and have taken nothing!" ~*Luke 5:5, KJV.*

Simon, in this statement, stands as an example of living by performance instead of faith. We can work and work trying to achieve righteousness and nothing comes of it! Faith is the opposite of works.

Simon's second statement spoke from Faith!

"Nevertheless at Thy word I will let down the net." ~*Luke 5:5, KJV*

Here Simon shows he is Simon Peter, the little stone. When Peter and his crew had Jesus on board and listened by faith, they caught "a great multitude of fishes..." Their catch nearly sank two ships. This is Glory and grace! When we see Jesus through His mighty power and love, like Simon, we too cry out, "O Lord!"

Jesus showed a picture to Simon and to those who read about this actual event. It is a prophetic message of Simon Peter's ministry! He became a fisher of men so great that he caught thousands of souls and pulled them in by the net (the gospel of Christ). Peter's ministry is still bringing in a mighty catch through the legacy of his apostleship and his written words in the Bible!

Hallelujah!

Have you noticed that those ministers who truly have the Spirit of Truth are teaching through their books or through preaching, those concepts that you, yourself, may have already received from the Lord? There have been many times I would have something planned for this book and I would hear a prominent minister repeat, almost word for word, what the Holy Spirit had taught me. I would actually get frustrated, saying to Jerry:"There he goes again!"

Laughing, Jerry would say, "That is exactly what you told me, word for word, what the Lord gave you!"

Then I would laugh too!

We have no time or right to be selfish or inclusive. For I know that every person who is open to the Lord's revelation is going to hear the same messages! The Words belong to the Lord! Not to us! And if enough voices are saying the same messages, the Word of the Lord will be sounded around the world by the trumpets of the Most High God!

Hallelujah!

Speaking of the "Spirit of Truth," "The Comforter," Christ says this:

"But when He, the Spirit of truth, comes, He will guide you into all truth. He will not speak on His Own; He will speak only what He hears, and He will tell you things yet to come . He will bring glory to Me by taking from what is mine and making it known to you. All that belongs to the Father is mine..." ~*John 16:13-15, NIVB*.

"...And everything that does not come from faith is sin." ~*Romans 14:23, NIBV*

Iniquity and sin is unbelief.

Does that mean that God does not give us any credit for all the "good things we do?" No, it means that the only good thing we can do is "believe"! God honors those who have faith in Him, those who believe in His loving kindness toward them, and those who share His love with others.

He honors us by unmerited favor!

He changes us from glory to glory!

He sets us with Him in High Places in Heaven!

He died and paid the ransom for every sin that we have and will commit in our lifetime!

He won for us the Kingdom of God that we might live and reign with Him! How can we be more honored than to reign with our God! Let's not compare the honor of men with the honor of God!

"For what saith the scripture? Abraham believed God, and it was counted unto him for righteousness." ~*Romans 4:3, KJV,*

"But we all, with open face beholding as in a glass the glory of the Lord, are changed into the same image from glory to glory, even as by the Spirit of the Lord." ~*2 Corinthians 3:18, KJV.*

"And God raised us up with Christ and seated us with Him in the heavenly realms in Christ Jesus, in order that in the coming ages He might show the incomparable riches of His grace. Expressed in His Kindness to us in Christ Jesus. For it is grace that we are saved, through faith-and this not from yourselves, it is the gift of God-not by works, so that no one can boast. For we are God's workmanship, created in Christ Jesus to do good works, which God prepared in advance for us to do." ~*Ephesians 3:6-10, NIVB.*

A dear friend of mine told me she had been at a worship service. The Spirit of the Lord fell on her.

Jesus said, "I love you more than anyone else in this room." She was troubled by such a thought and questioned it in her heart. Then the Lord said, "See that man over there? I love him more than anyone else in the room!" She relaxed; now she understood. Jesus loves each of us as if there is no one other person in His life. His love belongs to each of us, exclusively! His love is limitless! We have no need to feel left out.

11 HIS BOUNTIFUL GRACE

"So if someone is in Messiah, he is a new creation: the old things passed away, behold he has become new. And all things are from God...through Messiah" ~*2 Corinthians 5:17-18, NMB*

Living under grace rather than law is a new way of life! The attention we had on our own performance is shifted to Jesus' performance as a mighty God and His wonderful love for us!

Before grace, and under the law, our sins and our performance made us the center. But grace showcases Jesus' mighty works! Our heart is changed. We naturally have no desire to do anything but magnify Jesus! And we realize that all Jesus cares about is bringing us love, peace, and great joy.

One of my favorite quotes out of Mitt Jeffords' book <u>Journey to the Father's Heart</u> was what Christ told Mitt and Mitt's response:

"Mitt, I am not going to make you great and mighty in my sight, but I am going to become great and mighty in your eyes."

Mitt responded: "These were absolutely the most wonderful words I could have heard the Lord say because I knew that the only way that the Lord could become great and mighty in my sight was for Him to do great and mighty things for me." ~Mitt Jeffords,

God wants to do marvelous and mighty works for and in each one of us! He says that we need to seek for greater and greater miracles from Him. For He loves to delight us! Just ask.

"Call unto Me, and I will answer thee, and I will show thee great and mighty things which tho knowest not." ~*Jeremiah 33:3, KJV.*

One night a few years ago I knelt down in earnest faith. I was asking God to fulfill a prophecy which He had given to me. I was ready to "apprehend it."

While praying my mind was somewhat distracted with a vision. It was a vision of a mouth-watering grilled steak! I could even smell it!

I interrupted my praying by asking the Lord, "What is going on here? Is this the devil distracting me from this prayer that I am attempting to say?"

The Lord replied,"No, you have been on milk. Now I am going to put you on meat!"

Jesus said: "Labour not for the meat which perisheth, but for the meat which endureth unto everlasting life, which the Son of Man shall give unto you: For Him hath God the Father sealed." ~*John 6:27, KJV.*

Up until then, I had a vision or a message here or there. However, that very evening the Lord started me on the most exciting journey of my life! He directed me to some of Mitt Jeffords' revelations. He told me to study all them earnestly. I had not even heard of this man before seeing his name on a list of prophetic people. Yet, the Lord pointed him out to me: "He is the one!"

It became a marvelous in-depth study of the authentic Jesus. I spent hours at the computer getting to know the real Jesus that I had loved all my life! The revelations I found were so intense (yet so simple to understand) that I would have to get away from my computer and walk around to ponder what I had just read!

Mitt "proved" every revelation with many Bible

scriptures. Whether it is a vision or a revelation, there needs to be proof of its truth in the written word of God! It is even better if there are two or more witnesses from the Bible.

The Apostle Paul said to the Corinthians:"Every matter must be established by the testimony of two or three witnesses." ~*2 Corinthians 13:1, NIVB*

These new realities of Jesus were truly heavenly food and drink! I studied them constantly. My adoration of my Lord grew by leaps and bounds as I discovered His magnificent love.

My life changed dramatically. For example, I was able to turn the spirits of fear, dread, negativity, and condemnation over to the Lord. The Lord did the work of destroying them from my heart.

Finally, after months of studying and re-studying, the Lord said, "It is time to close on this study and start a new study."

I was looking at Christian music on You Tube shortly after that and the Lord said, "Look at this man's website!"

"What?" I asked." Lord, I have never heard of such a name! Smith Wigglesworth! "

He continued speaking and seemed to ignore my exclamation: "I want you to get his books and read them."

I began to ask my friends: "Have you ever heard of a man named Wigglesworth?"

Just a few had heard of him. I got on the web and ordered a number of his books. Wow! His books were filled with God's love. It was like reading beautiful scripture. I read several of them out-loud to Jerry. Smith Wigglesworth was truly an apostle of love and faith!

The Lord spoke prophetically through my husband and said, "There is a treasure trove of true revelations of Me given to men. You have the gift of discernment to know that which is true or not true!"

There are so many more that love the Lord and are blessed by His Spirit. The more we read other peoples visions, dreams, miracles, and revelations (Christ centered only), the more we learn how to exercise the gifts God has given us! It is like being given keys to open another precious part of our spirit!

No man or woman, however, is worthy of the highest position in our hearts. For the only One worthy of that place is Jesus. As you can see by reading this book, my greatest teachings have come from one-on-one conversations with the Lord Himself (through His Holy Spirit). We must always remember: Jesus' Holy Spirit is our best mentor!

Jesus said: "...These words you hear are not My Own, they belong to the Father who sent Me. All this I have spoken while still with you. But the Counselor, the Holy Spirit, whom the Father will send in My Name, will teach you all things and will remind you of everything I have said to you." ~John 14:24-26, NIVB

This new reality of Jesus positioned me to receive many more spiritual experiences. It was astounding what the Prince of Peace did one Wednesday evening! What happened was as real as I am sitting here typing the experience.

Jerry and I had been focused on the Lord most of that day. When we were ready to go to bed I said to the Lord, "Jesus, let me worship you through the night while I sleep!"

That is what I expected. Much to my disgust and disdain, however, debris of disconnected images of dark creatures and pictures marched through my mind's eye! My thoughts were, "What in the world is this about? I came to bed planning on worshiping Jesus and this disgusting stuff is running through my mind in a continuous stream."

Just as I was thinking that thought, I saw a whirlwind of white objects coming down from above me, and I decided to really focus on them in my spirit to see what they were! The whirlwind of white objects became dozens of white doves coming down and surrounding me!

I looked heavenward and saw Jesus smiling and releasing the birds from their cages. I am an artist, but the picture of the Lord releasing those doves was beautiful beyond reproducing.

He had on a simple robe of a light pastel aqua color. His robe came down just past His calves. On the bottom part of that simple garment was about an 8" metallic gold trim with embossed gold decoration on it. The cages were made of sticks fastened together.

My thoughts were, "How beautiful beyond description! Oh, that would be the most beautiful picture anyone could paint, if it were possible!"

Those Doves of Peace that Jesus sent to me worked, for as I focused on our Lord's beauty, I immediately went to sleep in a peaceful state that passes all human understanding.

I was not going to share this testimony, but the Lord urged me to share it because it is an example of His beauty and His love for us. Most importantly, it emphasizes that He is in fact the Prince of Peace and is capable of sending those White Doves of Peace to us in all our moments of need!

He told me later that if I desired to do so, I could send a spiritual white dove to those who need His peace just by decreeing it through the Holy Spirit! What a most wonderful God we worship!

God so loves us that He will bless us at the least little thing we ask Him to do for us and for others! His love is so great.

One day I was making a salad and kept hearing the theme song that the Lord had picked for me that day, "Holy Spirit Rain Down." It was constantly playing in my mind.

Then the Lord started speaking to me by His Holy Spirit. He told me to remember the twelve men who were sent out to investigate the land He had promised Israel. Two of them, Joshua and Caleb, believed it was possible to access God's Promises. They believed they could enter that particular territory and possess it, no matter how dangerous it was!

These same two knew they had a mighty God who would fulfill His vow. But the other ten saw only the pitfalls, were afraid, and did not truly believe they could occupy the land. Two believed! The rest of them doubted!

The two who believed were able to access God's promise! The rest of them died in their unbelief, without obtaining the inheritance—whereas they could have lived in the promised land had they chosen to believe! ~*Numbers Chapter 13*

"God is not a man, that He should lie; neither the son of man, that He should repent: hath He said, and shall He not do it? Or hath He spoken and shall He not make it good?" ~*Numbers 23:4, KJV*.

The Lord told me that we are in the same situation today. We have a choice! He said: "All of My children are the rightful heirs of My promises. Many of them fail to believe and press into them; therefore, they will die in their unbelief. But the children that press in with faith will receive those spiritual gifts and promises-because they believe!"

Salvation is given to all those who confess that Jesus died on the cross and was resurrected and accept His Lordship. The above paragraph is not talking about salvation but about receiving the full benefits of God's provisions already made for us!

The baptism of the Holy Ghost gives us the inheritance of the Kingdom of God and all its benefits and privileges. True believers in Jesus Christ can access the gifts of God. Only Believe! These are gifts for all believers, not just a few!

"And you also were included in Christ when you heard the word of truth, the gospel of your salvation. Having believed, you were marked in Him with a seal, the promised Holy Spirit, who is a deposit guaranteeing our inheritance until the redemption of those who are God's possession-to the praise of His Glory." ~*Ephesians 1:13-14, NIVB*.

"Abraham staggered not at the promise of God through unbelief, but was strong in faith, giving glory to God, being fully persuaded that what God had promised, he was able also to perform." ~*Romans 4:20, KJV*

"But now the righteousness of God without the law

is manifested…Even the righteousness of God which is by faith of Jesus Christ unto all and upon all them that believe…" ~*Romans 3:21-23, KJV*

12 HIS CROSS-OUR TRANSFORMATION

We cannot experience nor bask in the Glory of God until we embrace the cross of Jesus! For it is His love for us, shown at the cross, that transforms our lives.

"For the message of the cross on the one hand is foolishness to the lost! On the other hand, to those among us who are saved, it is the power of God!"~*1 Corinthians 1:18, NMB.*

"For I determined not to know anything among you except Jesus Christ and Him crucified."~*1Corinthians 2:2 KJV.*

December 26th: I had a gorgeous vision after Jerry and I retired for the evening. I was pondering on the gift, a crucifix, that I had given my son and daughter-in-law on Christmas Eve. [Note: a crucifix is a cross that has a sculpture-image of Christ on it.]

Throughout my life, the cross has been important to me. However, after I joined a traditional church organization at the age of 19, the cross moved to the background of my religious priorities. Crosses were not displayed prominently on the altar in many of their congregations. The blood of Jesus was not discussed often. Nevertheless, the Lord's Supper-Communion was considered very sacred!

Jerry and I have since left religion behind; consequently, the cross has become our mainstay and of great importance. The sacred sacrament of bread and wine as a remembrance of Jesus' sacrifice is taken frequently by us.

The work of God was finished on that cross!

"You (Jesus) are worthy to take the scroll and open its seals, because You were slain and with Your blood You purchased men for God from every tribe and language and people and nation. You have made them to be a kingdom and priests to serve our God and they will reign on the earth." ~*Revelation 5: 9-10, NIVB*, insert mine.

The cross is the symbol of Christ's victory over sin and death. The Lord pointed out that most people believe baptism washes away only their past sins. That's what I thought. Then the Lord corrected me, and said that the "remission of sin" spoken of in the scriptures means we are forgiven for the sins committed before we come to baptism, the sins the day of our baptism, and all the future sins—as long as we continue to believe in Jesus as our Savior.

In other words, all sin that was, is, and is to come has been paid for in full. It is a guarantee written and signed in heaven for every human being who wants to accept Christ's salvation for his or her own. I repeat, every sin was nailed to that cross-present, past, and future. He died once for all! When a sinner confesses and accepts Jesus as his/her savior, Jesus does not have to get back up on that cross again. The sin-debt has already been paid forever!

"...It is finished!" ~*John 19:30, NIVB*

"In Whom (Jesus) also we have obtained an inheritance, being predestinated according to the purpose of Him Who worketh all things after the counsel of His Own Will." ~*Ephesians 1:11 , KJV*, insert mine

Understanding this truism for the first time was exciting! I could barely contain myself! How wonderful is the love of God! Those who sincerely confess Him as their Savior become blessed beyond measure. We have an eternity to glorify and worship our God. It is not about earning or performing. It is living by faith! It is a life filled with unspeakable gratefulness, joy, peace, and love-glory

"But you are a chosen people, a royal priesthood (of believers), a holy nation, a people belonging to God." *~1 Peter 2:9, NIVB,* insert mine.

Jesus also died on the cross so our bodies could be healed as well. He hung on the tree, and now His broken body and His stripes are claim checks for our healing.

He alone paid the ransom!

Hallelujah!

As a child I was raised in a Protestant church where the cross was prominently displayed. However, the crucifix was considered a form of idolatry so it was shunned. But the newly-won freedom that Jerry and I now have has brought back a yearning for that old rugged cross. I began to desire to have a crucifix for our home.

I also wanted a crucifix for my son and daughter-in-law, not for an idol, but as a symbol of Christ's love. I ordered one for them online. When it arrived I was thrilled because it was so beautiful. The symbolism was even more beautiful. They were just as thrilled as I was!

As I mentioned earlier in this chapter, while pondering about the crucifix that I had given my son and daughter-in- law, I was immediately taken into a vision. Heavenly visions are always shown to me in the most breathtaking colors. This one was no less colorful. For in this vision I looked upon a crucifix that had a beauty I had never before imagined. The cross was a mosaic of intense, brilliantly-lit colors that looked alive. The image of Christ's body on the cross looked like pure gold!

Gold is a symbol of purity.

Then the most surprising thing happened: Christ's body instantly slipped out from under the golden image of Himself. Immediately following, I saw the real Jesus surrounded by a circle of adoring angels. I could only see His face because the arched wings of the angels blocked off the rest of Him from my view. He was happy and smiling at me. The complexion of Christ and that of the angels was past describing. It reminded me of the complexion of the children in Wm. Adolphe Bouguereau's paintings.

The angels' wings reflected soft colors like a pearl, yet their texture was soft and feathery. Such a sight, with their wings arched in perfect beauty and harmony! Ah, but the beauty of Christ's face superseded it all!

Christ is a living God! He did not remain on the cross or in the tomb. He was resurrected. He is the Resurrection! He ascended to sit on His throne on the right-hand side of the Father.

"Father...I have glorified Thee on the Earth, I have finished the work which Thou gavest Me to do and now, O Father, glorify Thou Me with Thine own self with the glory which I had with Thee before the world was." *~John 17:1, 4, 5, KJV*

One time the Lord explained, "Some of My children are put off by the cross and by My blood. They are ignorant or do not remember that the life is in the blood. To some the cross is even held up as a symbol of shame! To many, it is the end! It *was the end* of one covenant but *the beginning* of a new and Better one."

No greater Glory will you experience than when you embrace His cross! It is your privilege and choice to embrace the finished works of Jesus! If you have not accepted Jesus Christ as your Savior, you may confess Him now and enter in.

13 CHRIST: THE CROSS

Christ is a living God, mighty and strong! Yet so gentle and loving! He is absolutely adored by all the heavenly hosts and by all of us who know Him. Praise God above all heavenly hosts. Praise him all creatures here on earth as well. For He is the Lamb worthy to be praised!

HALLELUJAH!

How holy is our God! How great the condescension of God toward man: He willingly left His Throne and His beautiful home in heaven, and came down to earth in the form of a man to redeem us. He is Y'shua Messiah. He brought all men to salvation through that precious cross so they all might behold what true love is, even the true love of our God!

HALLELUJAH!

He hung on that cross and now we behold Him resurrected and coming in His glory. However, we will never forget the cross. His humility and His love won Him the prize and gift for us, those who believe in Him: the Kingdom of God!

HALLELUJAH!

For we are now, by that cross, citizens and heirs with Him; we are given all the rights and privileges of that citizenship. We, created and wonderfully made for Him, are partakers of His Glory-partakers of the great reconciliation between God and man! This is only possible by the blood of the Lamb which was bought and paid for us on the cross!

HALLELUJAH!

We, freed of all bonds, worship the Most High God for we are children of His. We, being therefore found perfect by Him and sanctified by His blood, that we need not fear. For even our bodies come under that precious grace, that precious cross, and that precious hope which we have in Him: Jesus the Christ, Y'shua Messiah, King of Kings, and Lord of Lords!

HALLELUJAH!

We have in Him: our healing, our sanctification, our righteousness, our freedom from all bonds (physically, mentally, and spiritually). In Him we have Eternal Life: "For in Him we live, we move, and we have our being." ~*Acts 17:28, KJV.*

HALLELUJAH!

He has borne every one of our sicknesses and our pains. Oh, He carried them for us. "He was wounded for our transgressions, bruised because of our iniquities." He took our chastisement Himself that we might find perfect peace in Him. We are healed by His wounds. ~*Isaiah 53:4-5, KJV,* paraphrasing by me

HALLELUJAH!

How could we ever turn away from that gift of healing which was so lovingly and freely given? Can we reject His sacrifice? Are we too proud to accept that which has been given to us by the glorious cross? I ask: How can we reject that which has already been died for, suffered for? I say, we cannot refuse!

HALLELUJAH!

Our mouths will not be closed, for we will praise His name! We will declare His goodness! We will decree His promises! We will not forget that sacrifice!

HALLELUJAH!

He is our God, forever and ever!

HALLELUJAH!

Amen.

14 THE NEW TESTAMENT

"I came to bring fire (the Holy Spirit Fire) upon the earth, and how I wish it were already kindled. But I have a baptism to undergo, and how distressed I Am until it is completed." ~*Luke 12:49-50, NIVB* inserts mine)

[Note: *I am going to paraphrase a lot of scripture. Most of this information is found in the precious book of Hebrews, Chapters 7-10. Due to space and the readers' patience, I will only touch some highlights. These are fundamental to the next chapters. This is a simple overview.*]

The placing of the name, "The New Testament" at the beginning of the second section of the Bible is somewhat misleading. The New Covenant was not instituted then, however, the "testator" of the New Covenant, Jesus Christ, was born at that time. During His ministry, Jesus operated under "the law."

Now Jesus was "made of a woman, made under the law, to redeem them that were under the law, that we might receive the adoption of sons." ~*Galatians 4:4-7, KJV.*

Until the time that Christ fulfilled the Old Covenant, there was chosen from among the Levitical/Aaronic priests one who would serve once a year as high priest. The tabernacle was built in such a way that only the high priest could enter the part which was called the "Holy of Holies." Death would immediately occur to anyone else who entered that room.

The high priest would enter the Holy of Holies on one special day, yearly, and offer a sacrifice of the blood of a goat for the forgiveness of the people and a bull for himself and his own household. ~*Leviticus 3:26;16:3-15* This event is known in Israel as Yom Kippur, the Day of Atonement, the tenth day of the seventh month of Tishri, (September–October). It was to atone for all of the sins of the entire Israelite community. ~*Leviticus 16:34*. Two Goats were chosen for the sacrifice. One goat would be taken for the sacrifice and the other goat (the scape goat) had the sins of all the people decreed upon him. The scape goat now burdened with all the sins of the people was led into the desert out of everyone's sight, taking with him the sins of the people.

The High Priest also offered a national perfect lamb on the Day of Passover. (These sacrifices will be discussed in more detail in my upcoming book,The Glorious Whore.)

God not only designed the tabernacle but the high priests garments as well. Exodus, Chapters 28, 35-40 contains the details of both of these. These chapters also reveal God as an artist, One who loves to create. He designed a richly decorated tabernacle with vibrant gold metalwork and colorful curtains. Everything was exquisite. Bright, colorful, and beautiful as well were the high priest's robe and accessories! Tinkling bells were attached to the bottom of his robe.

"And beneath upon the hem of it thou shalt make pomegranates of blue, and of purple, and of scarlet, round about the hem thereof; and bells of gold between them round about: a golden bell and a pomegranate, a golden bell and a pomegranate...And it shall be upon Aaron to minister: and his sound shall be heard when goeth in and unto the holy place before the Lord, and when he cometh out, that he die not." ~*Exodus 28:34-35, KJV*

This is the garb that the High Priest wore in the presence of the people. However, when he went in to sprinkle the blood upon the Mercy Seat he wore a simple white robe and necklace with a bell on it. He would rock back and forth so that the bell would ring as he performed his high priest duties in the Holy of Holies.

"And it shall be upon Aaron to minister: and his sound (bell) shall be heard when he goeth in unto the holy place before the Lord, and when he cometh out, that he die not." ~*Exodus 28:45, KJV,* insert mine)

The high priest was not allowed to sit down while in the Holy of Holies. This is consistent with the Old Testament and the Old Covenant. The high priest's work was never done. But in the New Covenant, Christ finished and fulfilled the works and office of the high priest and "sat down." He is now our Great High Priest forever!

"...When He had by Himself purged our sins, sat down on the right hand of the Majesty on high." ~*Hebrews 1:3, KJV*

The blood of bulls and goats, which the High Priest poured out on the "Mercy Seat," atoned for the people's sins for the previous year. There was a giant sized curtain-veil that separated the Holy of Holies from the rest of the tabernacle. This symbolized in a practical way that no one could approach God's Glory but the high priest.

Since the beginning of scripture, the sacrifice of the

Lamb foretold the sacrifice of the Perfect Lamb, Jesus! *~Genesis 4:4* This was the meaning of the old covenant. It clearly showed that people were unable by themselves to perform perfectly to obey the "law." Consequently, they needed a Savior, the Lamb of God!

Just as the Passover lamb's applied blood caused the "destroyer" to pass over each household, Christ's applied blood causes God's judgment to pass over sinners and gives life to believers.*~Exodus12:12,13,23; Romans 6:23; Hebrews 9:12*

These blood sacrifices in the temple were going on in Christ's lifetime. It must have seemed strange for Christ, knowing that these sacrifices foretold His own sacrifice as "the Perfect Lamb" on the cross.

The Old Testament religion went on even after Christ instituted another covenant and remains in a lesser sense today. The destruction of the temple in approximately 70 AD put a stop to the sacrifices of animals.

The members of the various religious groups of Judaism did not accept Christ as their Savior. Their traditions and precepts were constantly threatened by Him. Jesus told them:

"Do you think that I will accuse you to the Father: There is one that accuseth you, even Moses, in whom ye trust. For had ye believed Moses, ye would have believed Me: for he wrote of Me." ~ *John 5:45-46, KJV.*

The Old Testament, the Old Covenant, had to be fulfilled before a New Covenant could be made. Jesus fulfilled the Old Covenant by completing all its terms. He lived a perfect life, fulfilling every requirement. He spilled His blood. After the Old Covenant was fulfilled, He could freely institute another covenant.

"The former regulation (Old Covenant) is set aside

because it was weak and useless (for the law made nothing perfect). And a better hope is introduced, by which we draw near to God." ~*Hebrews 7:18, NIVB,* first insert mine, second insert theirs.

This New Testament only came into effect after the "testator" was dead: "Otherwise it is of no strength at all while the testator liveth." ~*Hebrews 9:16-17, KJV* The New Covenant could not be legal until after Christ's death!

At Christ's death, the veil of the temple was rent in two pieces, representing God's decree that Jesus was the last high priest forever. ~*Hebrews 7:17* He entered not the temple "made with hands" but into "Heaven itself" to sit on the right hand side of the Father! ~*Hebrews 9:24, KJV*

There was no more need for a high priest on earth to offer up sacrifices for the people.

Jesus was the Lamb that was slain! The veil was split! Man could enter into the Holy of Holies through the blood of the Only Begotten Son. Remember the following scriptures for they are tied in with the opening of the sealed book.

"No longer will a man teach his neighbor, or a man his brother, saying, 'Know the Lord.' Because they will all know Me, from the least of them to the greatest. For I will forgive their wickedness and will remember their sins no more." ~*Hebrews 8: 11,12 NIVB*

"Therefore He is able to save completely those who come to God through Him, because He always lives to intercede for them (as their High Priest)." ~*Hebrews 7:25. NIVB,* insert mine.

The synagogues, as already mentioned, went on functioning years after Christ's death. The Apostle Paul exclaims about the Old Law still being proclaimed years after Christ's death:

"But their minds were blinded; for until this day remaineth the same veil untaken away in the reading of the old testament; which veil is done away in Christ, But even unto this day, when Moses is read, the veil is upon their heart." ~*2 Corinthians 3:14-15, KJV,*

"Jesus has become the guarantee of a better covenant." ~*Hebrews 7:22, NIVB*

15 THE CUP!

What did Christ do that no man was able to do? Why was He the only one who could open the sealed book spoken of in Revelations 5? There were other men crucified. There were others raised from the dead. For example, Lazarus was raised from the dead, but not in an immortal body as was Christ. ~Taken from parts of "Revelation 5" by Mitt Jeffords, paraphrased by me

So what actually did the *Only Perfect Lamb of God* do? What made Jesus alone worthy to open the sealed book? I personally believe the answer lies in the contents of the cup which He alone was able and willing to drink. Only He loved His children enough to drink from that cup to save them.

So what was in that cup?

Jesus was not relishing drinking the contents of the cup but He was excited about the outcome. He spoke of the ordeal of His trial and crucifixion, saying: "I came to bring fire (The Holy Spirit Fire) upon the earth, and how I wish it were already kindled. But I have a baptism (what kind of immersion did He mean?) to undergo, and how distressed I Am until it is completed."~*Luke 12:49-50, NIVB,* inserts mine.

At the garden of Gethsemane Peter and the sons of Zebedee did not have a clue what was in the cup or that Jesus had come apart to prepare Himself for the dreadful event! For they fell asleep, unaware of what event was beginning to take place.

"Then cometh Jesus with them unto a place called Gethsemane, and saith unto the disciples, 'Sit ye here, while I go and pray yonder. And He took with Him Peter and the two sons of Zebedee, and began to be sorrowful and very heavy. Then saith He unto them, 'My soul is exceeding sorrowful, even unto death, tarry ye here, and watch with Me.'" ~*Matthew 26:36-39, KJV*

The very name Gethsemane gives us the very image of our dear Savior Jesus suffering for its definition is *olive press*. Olives were crushed in the olive crusher and then heavy stone slabs would be placed over the olives. The enormous weight would press out the oil. Here Jesus is, assailed by all the lies of the enemy and hordes of hell. His agony so great, our sins so heavy upon him so great that his blood was pressed from His body. His disciples had no clue.

"And He was withdrawn from them about a stone's cast and kneeled down, and prayed, saying, 'Father, if thou be willing, remove this cup from Me: nevertheless not My will, but Thine, be done.' And there appeared an angel unto Him from heaven, strengthening Him. And being in an agony He prayed more earnestly: and His sweat was as it were great drops of blood falling down to the ground." ~*Luke 22:41-44, KJV*

Days earlier the now sleepy sons of Zebedee had approached Him about a special favor for the two of them: "But Jesus said unto them, 'Ye know not what ye ask: can ye drink of the cup that I drink of? and be baptized with the baptism that I am baptized with?'" ~*Mark 10:38, KJV*

The *Cup* is spoken of in the Old Testament as containing the wrath of God. However, the wrath of God was only on those who were unrighteous! Jesus was perfect. But "the law worketh wrath: for where there is no law, there is no transgression." ~*Romans 4:15, KJV*

Now Jesus was "made of a woman, made under the law, to redeem them that were under the law, that we might receive the adoption of sons." ~*Galatians 4:4-7, KJV*

Jesus had to pay the price for our unrighteousness! He drank the cup of God's wrath for us! That was the Father and the Son's plan from the beginning of time.

Did Jesus drink the contents of the cup the moment the Father turned His back to Him? Was the Father, being a Holy God, unable to look upon the cross because the object of all man's sin was nailed to it?

"Thou art of purer eyes than to behold evil, and canst not look on iniquity..." ~*Habakkuk 1:13, KJV*.

Or was it when Jesus cried out: "Father, why hast Thou forsaken Me?" that the cup was emptied? For the Son had never been separated from the Father before. For the Son to be separated from the Father, even for an instant, was to be without life, without light, without love. It was about total isolation and separation. I have heard that is what hell is like.

People jokingly say that to go to hell where their buddies are is living it up. Sadly, through the testimonies of others, we discover one of the greatest torment in hell is that you are totally isolated from the love, light, life of God and from anyone else except the devil and hell's monstrous demons. You have only darkness and torment to exist in.

Jesus came so that none of us have to go there!

It is not He that puts us there: it is by our own

choosing! We need to believe in Jesus and confess His name, confessing that He was crucified and that He was resurrected. When we ask Him to come into our hearts, He is there with His arms open wide as we shout, "Daddy!"

"And everyone who calls on the name of the Lord will be saved." *~Acts 2:21, NIVB*

Hallelujah!

Where Jesus and the Father is, there is joy, peace, and love. The Father loves to see His children celebrate life and enjoy themselves! It is the devil who is the sad sack and who seeks to destroy our happiness.

Jesus said: "The thief (the devil) comes only to steal, to kill, and to destroy. I have come that they may have life and have it to the full. *~John 10:10, NIVB*, insert mine.

Jesus was isolated from the Father for *a moment* while on the cross. But because He walked that "valley" alone for us, we never have to be alone. We will never be isolated from the love of our Heavenly Father. Even if we choose to walk away, His love remains for us.

Many stand away from Him because they think that the Father could never forgive their *terrible sins*. But the Word says "that where sin abounded, Grace did much more abound." *~Romans 5:20 KJV*

One of the most famous and heart-rending parables in the Bible is one which I believe, we can all relate to in some way. The story is about a rebellious son, who after coming to the end of his own works, returns to his father. The most touching part of this story is that the father constantly watched for his son's return. When he saw his son "afar off," it says the father could not wait until his son reached him. The father ran to him and put his arms around his son. Nothing that happened in the past was important to the father. All he was focused on was "My son has returned to me!" ~*Luke 15:11-32, KJV.*

Believe this! God's love is so great that any one of us who remains in sin and darkness is in our Heavenly Father's heart and every heart beat! He is waiting for us to come home so He can run and throw His arms around us. Nothing of our past sins will He remember! Nothing could make Him happier than setting out a great banquet and feast just for us. We have all sinned and fallen short. Yet, He still stands with His arms extended to us, saying: "Run to Me, My child! I Love you! Come Now! Rush to the One Who loves you-even Y'SHUA MESSIAH!"~Taken from a message received by me

Oh, I finally get it! The cup was full of the wrath intended for us, the lawbreakers! This was a revelation to me-that without accepting Jesus as my righteousness, I remain a lawbreaker! I may try through my own strength to become perfect and righteous, but in doing so I am under the law and under the wrath! Therefore, I must assuredly accept His righteousness and His lordship as my own to be free from sin and wrath. By Jesus drinking that cup of wrath and becoming my righteousness; I have been changed from a lawbreaker to an adopted child of God!

"Much more then, being now justified by His blood, we shall be saved from wrath through Him." (Rom. 5:9, KJV)

It takes humility to accept that we are lawbreakers when we live by the law. But when we live by faith, we are no longer under the law, and therefore sin-wrath has no claim on us. It takes humility to receive our perfection from Jesus instead of earning it. But look at the reward! The reward is Jesus!

In Him is "all the Godhead..."~*Colossians 2:9, KJV* And therefore through Him residing now in us; we gain "the fullness of the Father!" ~*Ephesians 3:19, KJV*

"Therefore by the deeds of the law there shall no flesh

be justified in His sight: for by the law is the knowledge of sin. But now the righteousness of God without the law is manifested being witnessed by the law and the prophets. Even the righteousness of God which is by faith of Jesus Christ unto all and upon all them that believe: for there is no difference: For all have sinned, and come short of the Glory of God. Being justified freely by His Grace through the redemption that is in Christ Jesus." ~*Romans 3: 20-24, KJV*

"For since they do not know the righteousness of God but are seeking to make their own righteousness stand, they have not submitted to the righteousness of God." ~*Romans 10:3-4, NMB*

All the things we do from this point on are not to fulfill or obey a law. After we are baptized by the Holy Spirit, we are filled with God's love. God is no longer dealing with us as children of sin. He is dealing with us as His adopted children. Does that mean that we should sin? Apostle Paul said,"God Forbid!"~*Romans 6:15* (I will explain more about this in the following chapters.) But our very Spirit nature is changed to God's nature.

For like Jesus, we do not "live the rest of our earthly" lives "for evil human desires but rather for the will of God." ~Partial quotes from *2 Peter 4:2*

"For we are God's workmanship, created in Christ Jesus to do good works, which God prepared in advance for us to do." ~*Ephesians 3:10, NIVB*

"...But that no man is justified by the law in the sight of God, it is evident: for, The just shall live by faith. And the law is not of faith... Christ hath redeemed us from the curse of the law, being made a curse for us..." ~*Galatians 3:10-13, KJV*, capitalization theirs

One morning I was worshiping the Lord and basking in His Glorious Presence while walking on a country road.

"What is the worth of man? You ask." The Lord began to speak.

Father God says what is on His mind. Sometimes it is different than the topic you are interested in. He knows it is important for you to know. I love it!

"I created all things for a man to enjoy! I created a body for Myself and glorified Him! Knowing that man would fail and that man would fall, I sacrificed all including My Dear Son and caused Him to drink the dregs of wrath for you all! And He did it with joy! That is what man is worth! For He broke all the bands and broke down all the walls that separated you from Me. Now will you have full fellowship with Me?"

"Come!" He commanded me.

"Yes My Father, I will come! I will come to You! I will receive what you have and do offer me! For in Your presence alone is my fullness of joy! I covenant this day to be completely yours: shortcomings, faults, sins, doubts, lusts, and anything that keeps me from beholding you! I lay it all down at your feet. I am yours, I decree it, I promise and I am yours for ever!

16 THE SEALED SCROLL!

John the Revelator said, "...I looked, and there before me was a door standing open in heaven. And the voice I had first heard speaking to me like a trumpet said 'Come up here, and I will show you what must take place after this.' At once I was in the Spirit, and there before me was a throne in heaven with someone sitting on it. And the one who sat there had the appearance of jasper and carnelian. A rainbow, resembling an emerald, encircled the throne."~*Revelations 4:1-3, NIVB*

John's awesome experience plainly explains why everyone around the throne continues to say: "...Holy, Holy, holy is the Lord God Almighty, who was, and is, and is to come." ~*Revelations 4:8, NIVB*

"I will show you what must take place after this... " indicates John is going to experience an important event. He is going to experience that event in his spirit man instead of prophetic revelation. The event begins to be described in Revelations, chapter 5 of the Bible.

"Who was, and is, and is to come, " spoken of in the latter scripture, shows that time only exists in our world and not God's. Everything that takes place in heaven is present-tense. I smile as I think,"It will give us a headache if we try to figure that out!" John had this experience years later than the actual event took place, yet he was able to attend it as present time. Oh, how great is the mysteries of God and how hard to find out!

Hallelujah!

Mitt Jeffords, centuries later, was privileged to have the same experience as John. Mitt attended the event of the sealed book in present time!

[Note: As Mitt states in his writing; he was an avowed atheist until the Holy Spirit turned his life around. Then He was taught by Jesus and was told to record these revelations in detail. Mitt unselfishly shares his many visions, dreams, and experiences with others. This is fortunate for the rest of us who are Jesus-truth seekers. I have a personal testimony of the truthfulness of the revelations I have read, as they are confirmed by my own testimonies of Christ. You need to pray for your own confirmation.]

Mitt Jeffords relates: "Then the Lord said to me, 'All that which John witnessed in the Revelation, he did not see it by vision or by dream, but rather I took him in the spirit to the beginning where he actually witnessed Satan and his angels fall from heaven. *~Revelations 12:7-9* I also took John to the end where he witnessed the great white throne of judgment.'" *~Revelations 20:11-15*...Mitt Jeffords' quote from his "Revelation 5" writing.

As just mentioned, John received "the revelation of Jesus Christ" and Mitt Jeffords experienced the same Bible event in real time. The unsealing of the sealed book by Jesus in Revelations 5 is seldom discussed in Christian churches. This is extremely interesting as it is the very essence and primary purpose of the New Covenant-New Testament. It is phenomenal that over 100,000,000 or more could attend an event in heaven and it still be primarily ignored by

Christendom.

I *do not know* the exact sequence this event happened. It might have happened directly after Christ died on the cross or shortly after. Maybe it was immediately after He declared "it is finished" that His Spirit Man appeared in Paradise to open the sealed book! The evidence confirming when the event took place is His appearing as the "Lamb that was slain" to open the book. ~*Revelations 5:6, KJV* He told the thief on the cross, "I will be with you today in Paradise;" then he cried, "Father, into thy hands I commend my Spirit." ~*Luke 23:43,46, KJV*

The following seems to indicate it was after his trip to Hell. "Now that HE ASCENDED, what is it but that He also descended first into the lower parts of the earth? He that descended is the Same also that ascended up far above all heavens, that He might fill all things." ~ *Ephesians 4:8-10, KJV,* capitalization and emphasis theirs. Read also *1 Pet. 3:18-20.*

No matter when His first ascension as the Worthy Slain Lamb who poured out his own blood on the Mercy seat happened or when He opened the sealed book, the importance of both events seems to elude our traditional institutions. His resurrection experiences as recorded in the gospels get much more attention. It was three days after His death when He ascended at His resurrection. ~*John 20:17, KJV* This time whether the first or second time I do not know, His Spirit Man was encased by His immortal flesh. He did not allow anyone to touch Him until He had ascended to His Father in that state. His next ascension was after He came back to show His disciples He had been resurrected. ~*John 21:1, KJV*

Before His resurrection and opening of the sealed book, He descended into the spiritual prison-house (hell) and finished His work there. ~*1 Pet.18-20, KJV*. This is another aspect of His death and resurrection that is seldom spoken of in some Christian churches.

The innocent and perfect lamb of God had come forward willingly out of His Divine love to be the sacrifice for all men. The incarnate God was willing to suffer physically and spiritually for us in order that we might be reconciled to the Heavenly Father. He overcame death and hell and became our great High Priest to spill His own blood on the Mercy Seat in the Heavenly Holy of Holies.

"For Christ is not entered into the holy places made with hands, which are the figures of the true; but into heaven itself, now to appear in the presence of God for us:" ~*Hebrews 9:24, KJV*

He appeared and re-appeared a number of times during the forty days following His resurrection. His last recorded ascension was after teaching His disciples forty days just 10 days before Pentecost. ~*Acts 1: 1- 3, KJV*

But let us again consider in more detail the opening of the sealed scroll!

John saw a scroll in the right hand of the Father. It was written on both the front and back and sealed with seven seals. Then a question was shouted by a mighty angel,"...Who is worthy to break the seals and open the scroll? But no one in Heaven or on earth or under the earth could open the scroll..." ~*Revelations 5:1-3, NIVB*

John wept!

Jesus told Mitt,"When John wept, he was not weeping just for himself, but for all men; for seeing that there was no man in heaven, or on the earth, or beneath the earth that could be found worthy to take the book and remove the seals from off of it, he knew that man would forever continue in bondage to the darkness of his own ignorance, and not be allowed to enter into the kingdom of God. John wept because he knew that as long as the book remained sealed, then the truth about all things that pertain to the life of God would remain hidden from the eyes and the ears of man." ~*Revelations 5, KJV,* and *Revelation 5,* Mitt Jeffords

John knew that with Adam's fall, Adam had lost his own standing in God's kingdom. Adam also caused us to lose our place in God's kingdom. There was nothing but death and the spirit of darkness for mankind!Unhappiness, misery, and death are the end result of sin.

Only by the revelation knowledge of My truth shall the darkness of your ignorance perish and Satan's habitation be destroyed." ~*Revelation 5,* Mitt Jeffords

John wept. "Is there no one who can open the seals?"

God could not have unholy children in His Kingdom. He had created His children to reign over this earth before Adam fell. Reigning with the Only Begotten Son was only possible if the children were righteous. And they could only be freed from sin by the One who would pay the ransom for them. For they of themselves could never be free from sin.

John saw that unless the seals were broken off the Scroll we would be lost in the kingdom of darkness. Who was the one who could break the seals off and win the Kingdom for man?

"Then one of the elders said to me, Do not weep! See the Lion of the tribe of Judah, the Root of David, has triumphed. He is able to open the scroll and its seven seals." ~*Revelations 5:5, NIVB*

Then John "saw a Lamb, looking as if it had been slain, standing in the center of the throne...He came and took the scroll from the right hand of Him who sat on the throne." ~*Revelations 5:6-7, NIVB*

The twenty-four elders and the four creatures

fell down before the Lamb when they saw Him take the sealed book from the Father.

Only the Lamb, only Jesus was found worthy to stand "before the incorruptible God and then take the book that was sitting upon His lap. It was I, the Lamb of God, who all these heavenly creatures bowed before and worshiped, singing, "Worthy is the Lamb who was slain to receive power, riches, wisdom, strength, honor, glory, and blessings." ~*Revelations 5, KJV* and *Revelation 5*, Mitt Jeffords

"Then all the host of heaven fell upon their faces and worshiped the Lamb, for by His great love, He had been found worthy to win that which no man had ever won before, the power and the kingdom to win the hearts and the minds of man; the beloved of God. And they sung a new song, a song that could not have been sung before, saying, 'Worthy is the Lamb who took the book and opened the seals thereof'." ~*Revelations 5, KJV,* and *Revelation 5*, Mitt Jeffords.

"And they sang a new song, saying, You are worthy to take the scroll, and to open its seals: Because you were slain, and with Your Blood You purchased men (mankind) for God from every tribe and language and people and nation. You made them to be a Kingdom and priests to serve our God and they will reign on the earth"~*Revelations 5:9,10, NIVB,* insert mine.

Is this not Christ's greatest victory? Is this not our greatest gift won by His great love, body, and blood? Really, it 'boggles' minds to think of this! Whoever thought of such a thing! God, in the shell of human flesh, came to die so He could give His kingdom to His children-children who treated Him with such scorn, hatefulness, dishonor, and worst of all, children who murdered Him!

Jesus said: "For I did not win My Father's kingdom for Myself, for why would I win that which I previously had? I won My Father's kingdom for all those who would come to believe on Me, desiring for Me to be their Lord, their friend, their king, their brother, and their father. I won My Father's kingdom for those who allowed for Me to reign in their hearts and their minds with peace, and with truth, and with joy, and with wisdom, and with love." *Revelation 5*, Mitt Jeffords

Oh, Glory Hallelujah!

How can we help but leap about, sing, rejoice, and above all, delight in our KING OF KINGS!

"You made them (us) to be a kingdom and priests to serve our God and they (we) will reign on the earth" ~*Revelations 5:10, NJVB,* insert mine.

But what does all this mean?

It means that before Christ's finished works on the cross and His ascension to open the sealed book, man was lost. Because Adam had lost mankind's place in the kingdom of God, Christ had to come into man's realm to secure it again!

Before Christ opened the seals, God's Spirit Man could observe man, could talk with man, and could breathe spirit into man, but God's kingdom could not be in man! Angels of God could visit him. But there was no "comforter" dwelling in man; no baptism of the Holy Ghost! There could be mantles and anointing, but no kingdom of God inside a man. And there was no man inside God's kingdom! Jesus hinted at this to His apostles: "But you know Him, (The Spirit of Truth), for He lives with you and will be (future) in you . I will not leave you orphans. I will come to you." ~*John 14:17-18, NIVB,* insert mine.

Abraham looked forward to "his seed" (Jesus) who

would be a blessing to all nations! Isaiah spoke of the Christ profusely. The list of prophets who did so is long. The prophets of the Old Testament looked forward to this time of opening the seals. John was blessed to be there.

"But I tell you the truth: It is for your good that I am going away. Unless I do go away, the Counselor will not come to you: but if I go, I will send Him to you." ~*John 16:7, NIVB*

These were the words Christ Jesus spoke to His disciples before He went to His crucifixion. They were so sad to see Him go. We could, by looking at the befuddled lot, say that they felt the spirit of depression and abandonment. Jesus was well aware of their emotions and felt such compassion for them. He reassured them that this was best for them. He knew that the gift that He was going to secure for them would far outweigh the sorrow of the day.

"Father...I have glorified Thee on the Earth, I have finished the work which Thou gravest Me to do and now, O Father, glorify Thou Me with Thine own self with the glory which I had with thee before the world was." ~*John 17:1,4-5, KJV*

Christ said this to the Father earlier, "Father, glorify thy name." ~*John 12:28, KJV*

The Father answered, "'I have both glorified it, and will glorify it again.' The people therefore, that stood by and heard it said that it thundered..."~*John 12:28-29, KJV*.

If it were not for the event recorded in Revelation, Chapter 5 of the Bible, we would remain lost and fallen. Because of this event, the kingdom of the Living God resides in us! The Comforter can come! The Holy Spirit of Christ can now reside in us. The Father and the Son can come and 'sup' within us! Thus Revelation 5 caused the following passage to become a reality:

"The mystery that has been kept hidden away for ages and generations, but is now disclosed to the saints...the glorious riches of this mystery, which is Christ in you, the hope of Glory." ~*Colossians 1:26-27, NIVB*

God could not even come in and visit an unclean temple (our body) before Christ's sacrifice and the opening of the seals of the New Covenant. The New Covenant made us righteous and holy by Christ's righteousness and holiness. He did the work for us! I go into more detail about the baptism of fire that cleanses us in the following chapters.

"But you know Him (the Spirit of Truth) for He lives with ou and will be in you. I will not leave you orphans. I will come to you." ~*John 14:17-18, NIVB, insert mine.*

"And to know the love of Christ, which passeth knowledge, that ye might be filled with all the fulness of God." ~*Ephesians 3:19, KJV*

Mitt Jeffords, I am sure, could echo the words of the Apostle Paul, " For I neither received it of man, neither was I taught it, but by the revelation of Jesus Christ." (Gal.1:12, KJV)

Only through Jesus could this knowledge of God be revealed! Only through Him can we enter into the Father's presence! Only The Slain Lamb could unseal the true knowledge of God written in the sealed scroll! Only by The Word could the human body's veil of flesh and sin be split allowing Jesus, the King of Glory, to walk in and inhabit us!

"He that sees the truth of My word sees Me. He who sees Me also sees My Father. He that sees My Father overcomes the world and is made free from all of the powers of darkness." ~*Revelation 5,* Mitt Jeffords

The scroll itself was the knowledge of the life of God and His wonderful love! It ushered in the kingdom of God into our hearts.

The Father is a Spirit being!

Christ alluded to the Rev. 5 event in *John 4:23-24 KJV*. Jesus told the woman at the well "But the hour cometh, and now is, when the true worshipers shall worship the Father in spirit and in truth: for the Father seeketh such to worship him. God is a spirit: and they that worship Him must worship Him in spirit and truth."

Jesus, I believe, was referring to the same "hour" of His death and sacrifice when he also spoke to His disciples:

"Father, save Me from this hour: but for this cause came I unto this hour. Father glorify Thy Name." ~*John 12:27-28, KJV*

He was relating to the hour of His crucifixion followed closely by the release of the Father's spiritual kingdom into our hearts by the opening of the seals. It was then that the true worshipers could worship God in spirit and in truth.

"But when the fulness of the time was come, God sent forth His Son, made of a woman, made under the law, to redeem them that were under the law, that we might receive the adoption of sons. And because ye are sons, God hath sent forth the Spirit of His Son into your hearts crying, Abba, (Daddy), Father. Wherefore thou art no more a servant, but a son; and if a son, then an heir of God through Christ." ~*Galatians 4:4-7, KJV,* insert mine.

"It was when I was found worthy to take the scroll and open it that My heavenly Father gladly gave to Me His prize, His entire heavenly kingdom, as well as the fullness of His power, His riches, His wisdom, His strength, His honor, His glory, and His blessings." ~*Revelations 5:12 and Chapter 10,* Mitt Jeffords.

What was in the scroll or book? God's Spirit of love and truth! The Father's life! The scroll may have also been as simple as a contract for the New Covenant.

Let's break down the scriptures and revelations into parts to understand what this is all about!

Who was the "testator" who fulfilled the contract : "It was when I was found worthy" indicates that Jesus fulfilled all the terms of the New Covenant-contract. So the deed was handed over to Him.

Who was the Grantee of the deed:"My heavenly Father." What was the warranty deed for: The Father's "prize, His entire heavenly kingdom, as well as the fullness of His power, His riches, His wisdom, His strength, His honor, His glory, and His blessings." ~*Revelations 5:12, KJV, Chapter 10*, Mitt Jeffords.

What were the terms to be sealed with? Death to the testator:

"With Your Blood You purchased men (mankind) for God." ~*Revelations 5:9, NIVB*

Who else won something with this New Contract : "I won my Father's kingdom for those who allowed for me to reign in their hearts and their minds...and if a son, then an heir of God through Christ." ~Chapter 10, Mitt Jeffords

Why was the Father so "glad" to give this prize to His Son, since His Son had the kingdom already?

"Because ye are sons, God hath sent forth the Spirit of His Son into your hearts crying, Abba, (Daddy), Father." ~*Galatians 4:6, NIVB*, insert mine.

The Father always wanted a family! Each time we say, "Daddy," it thrills the Heavenly Father!" This was the Father's plan from the beginning! He has foreknowledge! Time is only with men, not with God. There is no mystery for Him. He sees all and knows all. He knew that Adam and Eve were going to fall. But He knew love meant nothing if received from performing robots.

Therefore, He gave them freedom of choice! He created a body for Himself-His Only Begotten Son before creation so that He could win back His children after *the fall.*

"With Your Blood You purchased men (mankind) for God." *~Revelations 5:9. NIVB,* insert mine

Christ paid the price so that now the Father's fallen children could be made righteous through the righteousness of His Only Begotten Son, and now they could belong to the Father as well as the Son.

Christ had won back what Adam lost for us. Through the blood of Jesus, all who will believe in Jesus has been reinstated as a son of God made to reign and to put all things under his feet as did Jesus.

"For this purpose the Son of God was manifested, that he might destroy the works of the devil." *~1 John 3:8, KJV*

"Because as He is, so are we in this world." *~1 John 4:17, KJV*

Now the fullness of the Father could be in the adopted children as well as the Son. Because the Son gave mankind His righteousness as a gift if they would only believe (have faith) in Him and choose Him as their Savior so that "we might receive the adoption of sons." *~Galatians 4:5, KJV*

Jesus declared: "My heavenly Father gladly gave to Me His prize, His entire heavenly kingdom, as well as the fullness of His power, His riches, His wisdom, His strength, His honor, His glory, and His blessings." *~Revelation 5,* Mitt Jeffords

Glory Hallelujah! We cannot begin to Honor and Praise our God enough! "Holy, Holy, Holy is the Lord God Almighty!" *~Revelations 4:8, KJV*

Now the King of Kings declares victoriously, "I was dead, and behold I am alive forevermore, and I have the keys of death and of Hades." *~Revelations 1:18, KJV*

17 THE FAN AND THE FIRE

A tanned, handsome man was standing with his back to me. The colors of this mini vision were beautiful. It was like looking back into time because of his clothing. He was bare down to his waist. His white short skirt could have been used as a costume for a Biblical Harvester on a movie set! His arm bracelet looked like braided green, red, and gold. The large fan he held in his hand was made of very long, fluffy, white feathers. It was a sharp contrast to his dark tan.

The vision came and went so quickly that I did not have time to really take in all the details. I said to Jerry, "I just had a quick vision and I have no idea what it means. I know that the Lord will show me later. It was beautiful!" I described it to Jerry, and he did not understand the meaning of the vision either. Little did I know the Lord was preparing me for a chapter I was going to write in a few weeks-specifically this one.

After this vision and while editing earlier chapters, I noticed a scripture that I had already placed in one of them. I could barely contain my joy as I recognized the man with the fan in His hand. The Lord opened my eyes! For when I originally selected *Matthew 3*, I had not noticed Him. In fact

I have just now moved that particular scripture to this chapter.

John the Baptist spoke these words:

"I indeed baptize you with water unto repentance: but He that cometh after me is mightier than I, whose shoes I am not worthy to bear: He shall baptize you with the Holy Ghost, and with Fire, whose fan is in His Hand, and He will thoroughly purge His floor, and gather His wheat into the garner, but He will burn up the chaff with unquenchable fire." ~*Matthew 3:11,12 KJV*

Days earlier as I began to plan for this chapter, I was looking for some insight from the Holy Spirit on which scripture to use. I studied the verse again, and "Hallelujah," its message became clear. John is not talking about Jesus purging the world; he is talking about Jesus baptizing us with the Holy Ghost and fire. Nowhere in the previous verse is there any indication of a different context than this.

"When He had by Himself purged our sins, (He) sat down on the right hand of the Majesty on high." ~*Hebrews. 1:3 KJV*, insert mine)

Our spirit man or core has to be purged by the Holy Ghost Fire before God can make us His abode, or the place where He lives and reigns. Jesus does the work of purging, not we ourselves. He, Himself, makes us perfect. He comes in and circumcises our hearts, cutting away all the dark stuff. We cannot do it of ourselves because we are flesh! God cannot live in unholy places, so He uses the fire of the Holy Ghost to cleanse us. Our inner core is no longer an enemy to God, as it was before our spirit man was transformed.

Now in this context let us review the above noted scripture.

"He shall baptize you with the Holy Ghost, and with "Fire," Whose fan is His Hand, and He will thoroughly purge

His floor, and gather His wheat into the garner, but He will burn up the chaff with unquenchable fire."~*Matthew 3: 11,12 KJV*

Oh, how great is our God, for after we are immersed in the water as a burial to our sin, we are "born anew." He gives us the baptism of the Holy Ghost and the Fire. He is the harvester with the fan! The floor of our inner core, our spirit, now belongs to Him because of our confession of faith! Our inner core is now His floor. The wheat is "the finished victorious works" of Jesus. Christ's Holy Spirit gathers His finished works into the "barn," (our individual temple), where His Kingdom now resides.

"So if someone is in Messiah, he is a new creation: the old things passed away, behold he has become new. And all things are from God...through Messiah." ~*2 Corinthians 5:17-18, NMB*

The Holy Spirit of Christ, after "gathering" the good fruit, gathers all the bad "chaff" the devil has planted in our hearts, and burns them up with the Fire of the Holy Ghost. Until the time we have this "born again Spirit," the devil is free to walk around in our temples. But when Jesus abides in us, on the throne of our hearts, the devil is disarmed and "burned out." God cannot inhabit a temple made or purged by "human hands." ~*Acts 7:48* Then He seals this perfect new spirit that He has put in us forever. We become His property and He locks the barn door! We are His!

"A people that has become God's property, so that you would proclaim the manifestation of divine power." ~*1 Peter 2:9 NMB*

"Ye were sealed with that Holy Spirit of promise." ~*Ephesians 1:13, KJV*

Whoever thought of such a thing?

"How shall not the ministration of the spirit be rather glorious?" ~*2 Corinthians 3:8 KJV*

I repeat these verses:

"He shall baptize you with the Holy Ghost, and with "Fire," Whose fan is His Hand, and He will thoroughly purge His floor, and gather His wheat into the garner, but He will burn up the chaff with unquenchable fire." ~*Matthew 3: 11,12 KJV*

"When He had by Himself purged our sins, (He) sat down on the right hand of the Majesty on high." ~*Hebrews 1:3 KJV,* insert mine)

A scripture found in the third chapter of Malachi relates and corresponds perfectly with theses same two verses found in Matthew 3, which is about Jesus with the fan.

The messenger preparing the way of Christ is John the Baptist. Then Christ "shall suddenly come to his temple (our spirit core)...even the messenger of the covenant (new covenant-baptisms of water and Holy Spirit), whom ye delight in; behold He shall come, saith the Lord of Hosts. But who may abide the day of His coming? and who shall stand when He appeareth? for He is like a refiner's fire, (Holy Ghost Fire) and like a fullers' soap: And He shall sit as a refiner and purifier of silver; and He shall purify the sons of Levi, and purge them as gold and silver, that they may offer unto the Lord an offering in righteousness." ~*Malachi 3:1-3 KJV,* inserts mine

Remember the sons of Levi were the priests in the temple, but after Christ came, the Law of Moses was fulfilled and the temple's veil was rent!

"You made them (us) to be a kingdom and priests to serve our God and they (we) will reign on the earth" ~*Revelations 5:10, NJVB,* insert mine

The Law of Grace replaced the Law of Moses and the born again Christians replace the Levite Priests. Therefore He is again referring to the work of Christ in us, His temples!

The only offering we have in righteousness is Christ's righteousness: His faith and our belief in His shed blood for our sanctification. Glory to Him alone!

"Ye also as lively (living) stones, are built up a spiritual house, an Holy Priesthood." ~*1 Peter 2:5, KJV,* insert mine

The Lord spoke to the Levites and now to us: "I Am their inheritance...I Am their possession." ~*Ezekiel 44:28 KJV*

The Lord is constantly teaching and purging!

Hallelujah!

I have discovered the simplest of truths. "The Kingdom of God" is anywhere God reigns.

That is why Jesus said, "The kingdom of God does not come by your careful observation, nor will people say, 'Here it is' or 'There it is,' because the kingdom of God is within you." ~*Luke 17:20-21, NIVB*

In the natural man we see the kingdoms of the world as having boundaries. China built the great wall so we could recognize the borders of China's kingdom. With our natural mind when we thinks of China, we picture that particular chunk of territory. We do the same with God's kingdom. In our mind we picture the Lord has a certain territory staked out in heaven where His kingdom is. However, remember God is much higher than our thoughts are. Wherever Father God reigns, it becomes His kingdom. The universe is His kingdom. It is not contained by walls or sides like a box of dry cereal.

New Jerusalem coming down is a city prepared for people who are reigned by God. But He is not limited to a city. When we choose Him as Lord over our life, His kingdom is in us! When we are born again by water and the Holy Spirit, it is said of us that we have the Kingdom of God residing in us! We choose who will reign in the Kingdom of our heart.

A couple of years ago I had a spiritual dream. In this dream, I saw a small group of tiny miniature people milling around. I could see that they were dressed in ordinary garments.

While still in this dream, I was directed by the Lord's voice back to a dream I had received earlier-an earlier dream which in my conscious mind I could not recall having! However, the Lord recalled it clearly to me. (It was a dream within a dream!)

In the dream that the Lord brought back to my memory, there was a really large group of tiny people milling around. They were dressed in the finest clothing and had crowns on their heads and appeared as though they were kings of some kingdom. There was a sharp contrast between them and the few people dressed in ordinary clothing that I had seen at the beginning of my dream vision.

I awoke and after pondering it for a short time, the Lord said "These people in kingly garbs are those things that I have removed from your heart. You still have a few, but they are no longer kings and have been made humble in your heart."

I asked what some of those kings represented, which had held high positions in the kingdom of my heart. He told me that some were long held views that I have had, such as traditions and precepts of men. I asked Him what the few remaining ordinary dressed people were.

"Some," He said, "were feelings of guilt for sins which had been forgiven but which I had not forgiven myself for.

Some were views which were not held as important to me...thus they were dressed in ordinary clothing."

I was very humbled to think that my God and Savior had condescended to save and cleanse my heart of things that I could not get rid of myself! I just praised Him all morning for setting me free!

Once during a worship service in our home church group, I saw this little pure white lamb appear! It was just running and stopping in front of our group, who were worshiping in a circle. I had always thought of Jesus as a full grown ram! So it surprised me that this one was so tiny! Jesus comes as both the Lamb and the Lion into our hearts, but we must invite Him in.

One evening I was visiting with the Lord, as I often do, and He asked me, "You have known me as the Lamb, but have you known Me as the Lion of Judah?" (He knew the answer, but He wanted me to think about it!)

I thought and quickly answered, "Yes, Lord, for You were the Lion of Judah while cleaning out the dark areas of my heart. You have been and continue to attack ferociously all my fears, my judgments, my wanting to be right and correct, and my natural reasoning!"

Listening to praise songs always brought Jerry and me right into worship. Many times the Holy Spirit accessed our spirit through words or visions during these times. For example, one day while worshiping the Heavenly Father, the Holy Spirit fell upon us in abundance. I looked up to the Throne Room and I saw what I did not expect. I saw the Lion of Judah resting confidently before the Throne. I could feel love emanate from Him. In a friendly tone He roared, " I AM CAPABLE!"

He is so beautiful! He is a huge lion that looks like He has just been groomed by ministering angels! The open vision was as clear as a movie picture only brighter! As Jerry and I were moving around the sanctuary praising the Lord, Jerry felt the presence of the Lion of Judah walking beside him.

He, the great I Am, the Lion of Judah roars, "I Am capable!"

If you have any issues, you may desire the Lion of Judah to come into your heart to ferociously attack all the doubts that still remain in your heart and mind! Allow Him access to fight your battles! None of us can do this work, only Jesus can fight our battles for us! Invite Him now, as the Lion of Judah to come into your heart!

"Behold, the Lion of the tribe of Judah, the Root of David." ~Revelation 5:5 KJV

18 THE WAY OF HOLINESS

One day I was visiting with Jesus. I found myself in an open vision. I was standing looking out over a flat, barren desert. I could see miles of dry parched land in all directions. Strange as visions can be, I saw a wrought iron chair sitting there in front and to the left of me. When I walked around it and sat down, the Lord told me that *my sitting down* represented *my resting in Him.* The minute I sat down, fountains of living water broke forth all over that wasteland. Streams and rivers were formed before my eyes. It was beautiful and wonderful to behold. It is glorious to experience Him in such a way. You can also experience Him.

Hallelujah! Our God is an awesome God!

"There remained therefore a rest to the people of God. For he that is entered into His rest, he hath ceased from his own works as God did from His. Let us labour therefore to enter into that rest, lest any man fall after the same example of unbelief." ~*Hebrews 4:9-11, KJV*

"Grace and peace be multiplied unto you through the knowledge of God and of Jesus our Lord, according as His divine power hath given unto us all things that pertain unto life and Godliness, through the knowledge of Him that has called us to Glory and virtue...For if these things be in you, and abound, they make you that ye shall neither be barren nor unfruitful in the knowledge of our Lord Jesus Christ." ~*2 Peter 1:2-3 and 8, KJV*

I had planned to share the above vision with you; however, I had chosen a different title for this chapter. The first title I had chosen just did not seem right so I deleted it. Immediately on doing so, the Lord said," THE WAY OF HOLINESS is the name it should be called."

And I said, "Okay."

Then I pondered about how that title was going to go with the message and visions I had planned for this chapter. "So," I thought, "Jesus wants this chapter to be about holiness." I began free lancing on holiness. But that was not successful, so I decided I would start with my vision of the desert. I could add what Jesus wanted given before it or after it in the chapter.

My grandson, Alex, immediately saw a connection between the title and the vision. He said, "With Christ in your heart there is life, and without Him there is nothing but barrenness and death."

Alex certainly gave a true statement. Jesus is "the Way, the Truth and the Life." ~*John 14:6, KJV*

A concordance on the scriptures is invaluable! Mine is falling apart from use! Looking for proof of this vision and "The Way of Holiness,"I discovered a scripture that absolutely astonished me! I will quote part of it but please read it all:

*"The desert and the parched land will be glad...*Then will the eyes of the blind be opened and the ears of the deaf be unstopped. Then will the lame leap like a deer, and the mute tongue shout for joy. *Water will gush*

forth in the wilderness and streams in the desert. The burning sand will become a pool, the thirsty ground, bubbling springs. The haunts where jackals once lay, grass and reeds and papyrus will grow. *And a highway will be there. It will be called The Way of Holiness! ~Isaiah 35:1, 5-8, NIVB*

The parts that I have emphasized in the above scripture are exactly what I saw in my vision! And this verse also speaks of "The Way of Holiness," which Jesus gave me for the title of this chapter!

What is this walk, this way of holiness? Jesus is the "Way of Holiness!"

"Come unto Me, all ye that labour and are heavy laden and I will give you rest. Take My yoke upon you, and learn of Me; for I Am meek and lowly in heart: and ye shall find rest unto your soul, For my yoke is easy, and my burden is light." *~Matthew 11:28-30, KJV*

In this "Way of Holiness," do we sometimes look at our circumstances and see barrenness and spiritual dryness? If we *rest* in Jesus and turn our eyes upon Him, everything will be changed at the blink of an eye. Living Water will come out of fountains, streams, and even our belly!

This is true as shown in the following scripture.

Jesus says: "If anyone is thirsty, let him come to Me and drink. Whoever believes in Me, as the scripture has said, streams of Living Water will flow from within him." *~John 7:37-38, NIVB*

The King James Version says, "Out of his belly shall flow rivers of Living Water."

Maybe my vision is about what Jesus says to us as He said to His disciples:"Take time out of your busy schedule and your responsibilities and rest in Me." (Paraphrased by me) Jesus said, "Come ye yourselves apart into a desert place, and rest a while...for there were many coming and going, (needing to be ministered to) and they had no leisure so much as to eat." ~*Mark 6:31, KJV*, insert mine

But I think it has even a deeper meaning, although these truths are all part of it!

My husband Jerry and I were volunteer chaplains at a local hospital. One morning I was awakened at 3:00 a.m. from a spiritual dream. In the dream, Jerry and I were laying hands on people and giving them prophetic blessings, like we did already in our virtual hospital ministry. In my dream I was speaking this message:

****

"And this is the angels' message that we bring to you- tidings of great joy!

JESUS BIRTHED IN US!

That we may become righteous as He is righteous! Not by our own works, lest we should boast of ourselves, but by His righteousness in us, His condescension to us, that by His stripes we are healed-freed of all sin by His blood.

For this too is our message: He was crucified for our sins, suffered for our mistakes, causing us to rise up into Himself to be transformed daily into His likeness so we might partake of His presence though still living on this earth. Daily being transformed-changed from glory to glory! And He taking us into His arms, lifts us to sit in heaven's high places! That we, too, might sit upon His throne with Him! For He won the Kingdom for us that He might share a life of wonderment and love with us, His children!

Who has heard of such a thing? To whom has such a report been made? *Jesus, King of glory, birthed and living in us! Hallelujah!*

This is the true angels' message. These are the true tidings of great joy! Amen." (End of Dream)

****

Father God will give to each of us "according to the riches of His glory, to be strengthened in power by His Spirit working in your inner man, to make Messiah live in your hearts through faith, when you have been rooted and established in love, so that you would be able to seize, with all the consecrated ones, what is the breadth and length and height and depth, and to know the love of the Messiah that surpasses our knowledge, so that you would be filled with all the fullness of God." *~Ephesians 3:16-19, NMB*

The "Way of Holiness" comes in full fruition into our lives when we are born anew! The baptism of the Holy Ghost changes us forever. "Jesus birthed in us!"

Jesus said: "Marvel not that I said unto thee, 'Ye must be born again. The wind bloweth where it listeth, and thou hearest the sound thereof, but canst not tell whence it cometh, and whither it goeth: so is every one that is born of the Spirit.'" *~John 3:7-8, KJV*

Early Easter Sunday morning, 1991, while Jerry and I were staying with my brother-in-law and sister who lived near Council Bluffs, Iowa I received the baptism of the Holy Ghost and fire! It happened in a spiritual dream vision. What was so very strange is that my husband was in the same dream vision with me, literally! One thing I know is that God is sovereign over all of creation and nothing is impossible or difficult for Him.

Sometimes in my spiritual dreams, I am an Indian woman wearing a white buckskin dress with decorative, blue beads on it. That is how I was dressed in this dream. I was with a tribe of Native Americans who were sitting on benches. I arose from the bench I had been sitting on and went alone out into the middle of a green pasture or meadow. All of the tribal members were looking on as if it was some kind of an event or rite of passage.

Then the oldest looking man I had ever seen, wearing a breech-cloth, appeared in the middle of the pasture also. He looked ancient to me! His face was weathered and wrinkled, and his body was like skin wrapped over bones.

I stood before him. With both hands, he raised a clay tablet above his head. The clay tablet was about 8" x 12." The sides were actually curved toward each other slightly. As I looked upon the tablet, I immediately recognized the symbol of the Holy Ghost.

Then the Holy Ghost overpowered me, and I instantaneously dropped to my knees. I was totally engulfed in the Spirit of God as it poured out in waves over me. When it subsided I got back up, and again I looked upon the symbol. Even more powerfully did the Holy Ghost baptize me the second time. I dropped down to the ground. Waves and waves of the Holy Ghost passed around and through me. It was overwhelming and marvelous! I had experienced the Holy Ghost before, but nothing compared to this time! Then the vision closed.

I woke up at the same time my husband awoke and I said, "What a fantastic dream experience I had!"

He said, "So did I!"

I relayed my dream to him.

Jerry said,"I know what happened because I was

there! I was with the tribe watching from a distance."

He reiterated what the ancient Indian man looked like. He told me that when the man raised the clay tablet, a light came from above. The light was so powerful that the whole tribe fell down face first to the ground. Even though they were some distant away, they could not look. That is the power of the Fire of the Holy Spirit. That is the Shekinah Glory burning in us.

Why would any of us prefer to live a life without the baptism and life of the Spirit? What happens to us becomes a key to unlock the faith of others. *Our experiences are not to lift us up but to encourage others on their spiritual journey! So please share!* Our experiences are to show "the Way of Holiness," as revealed through Jesus! The words of the Holy Bible can be accessed virtually in our lives through apprehending (reaching out and receiving) them through faith! For example, *the things I experience, you can too—if you yield yourself completely to the Lord.* It is about having a close relationship with the Lord Jesus Christ, whose Spirit lives in those who are born again!

"Jesus answered and said unto him, 'Verily, verily, I say unto thee, except a man be born again, he cannot see the kingdom of God.'" *~John 3:3, KJV*

Jesus may communicate with you by vision or prophetic word-teaching you, when you really are not expecting it. Sometimes you can even be doing something else. For example, I had another wondrous vision! I wrote down the date later that same day, January 3, 2013. How could I ever forget that date?

My husband and I were at the hospital literally, prophetically praying, and blessing people. We had just left a patient's room when the Lord began speaking to me and brought up a subject that was separate from what we were doing. He told me marriage takes place between Him and us when His Spirit intertwines with ours; that is when we become one with Him. Like He is one with the Father. Then His righteousness becomes our righteousness, His perfection becomes our perfection, and even His faith becomes our faith. This is "resting" in Him. This is "the Way of Holiness!"

"But the one who is joined to the Lord is one spirit with Him." ~*1 Corinthians 6:17, KJV*

"I pray for them all to be joined together as one even as You and I, Father, are joined together as one. I pray for them to become one with us... You live fully in Me and now I live fully in them so they will experience perfect unity..." ~*John 17:21,22 TPT*

I asked the Lord, "Why are you bringing up this now?" Since we were in the process of praying for people. He answered me in a vision. I entered the break room at the hospital shortly after and immediately was in an open vision and I was dressed in a wedding dress and Jesus was in an indescribable wedding garment. I had my arm in His and we were radiantly happy beyond this earthly life. Later I found out that some others had had a similar experience.

"Therefore, my brethren, you also have become dead to the law through the body of Christ, that you may be married to another-to Him who was raised from the dead, that we should bear fruit to God."~*Romans 7:4 NKJV*

The key to having a close relationship with Jesus is in a marriage! When you have a great marriage, it will probably be evident that you enjoy sharing, visiting, and being with each other. We especially like being complimented and appreciated! I adored my husband and he felt the same about me. We loved being with each other constantly. We were truly "one" in more ways than just physical. We were best friends. So it is with Jesus!

I repeat, "But the one who is joined to the Lord is one spirit with Him." ~*1 Corinthians 6:17, KJV*

"Whosoever shall confess that Jesus is the Son of God, God dwelleth in him, and he in God. And we have known and believed the love that God hath to us. God is love: and he that dwelleth in love dwelleth in God, and God in him. Herein is our love made perfect, that we may have boldness in the day of judgment; because as He is, so are we in this world." ~*1 John 4:15-17, KJV*

"For He hath made Him to be sin for us, who knew no sin; that we might be made the righteousness of God in Him ." ~*2 Corinthians 5:21, KJV*

"That Christ may dwell in your hearts by faith, that ye, being rooted and grounded in love...to know the love of Christ, which passeth knowledge, that Ye might be filled with all the fullness of God." ~*Ephesians 3:17,19, KJV*

I was awakened early one morning about 3:00 a.m., so I knew the Lord wanted me to spend some time with him. I had been studying some scriptures about the love of the Father for His children. All at once I was experiencing His love abundantly. I had always known and experienced Jesus dwelling in me by the Holy Spirit; however, this was just one of those moments which defy all thought! It was as if Jesus Himself had jumped into my skin! My mind was thinking not about Jesus but as Jesus! My love was actually His love. My thoughts were like His! I had never experienced anything like it before! My mind had literally and totally surrendered to the Mind of Christ. The minute my own thoughts barged in it ended! Oh, how I regretted getting into my intellect and analyzing it!

I had read about such experiences and had desired the same. I smile now as I write this; things do come suddenly! It always comes when you are not expecting it! This experience defied even my imagination!

Our Spirit man is one with the Spirit of Truth-Holy Spirit of God, however our mind is part of our Soul. We need to "renew our mind" so that it is totally surrendered to the Mind of Christ. We do this by submitting our mind to the guidance of the Holy Spirit which is in us. The Lord once enlightened me to know that the mind of Christ is the Holy Spirit. So when we say we have the mind of Christ we are saying that we have the Holy Spirit dwelling in us and directing us.

"Know ye not, that ye are the temple of God, and that the Spirit of God dwelleth in you?" ~*1 Corinthians 3:16, KJV*

I wept to think of the condescension of God! It humbled me so to think that my God, my Savior would come and dwell in me. I wept that He should love so greatly and desire so deeply to have true companionship with us and that the fullness of the Godhead dwells within us!

"For in Him (Christ) dwelleth all the fullness of the Godhead bodily. And you are complete in Him, which is the Head of all principality and power." ~*Colossians. 2:9-10, KJV*, insert mine

Who ever thought of such a thing?

Who could have imagined such a love as our Father has for us? He condescended to die on the cross to win the kingdom for His children, and now He is to dwell fully in us! That is a love that no man has a concept of or a word to describe! Truly He has "borne our griefs and carried our sorrows." ~*Isaiah 3:4, KJV* And now He cleanses us so that He might dwell within us!

"I pray that out of His glorious riches He may strengthen you with power through His Spirit in your inner being, so that Christ may dwell in your hearts through faith." ~*Ephesians 3:16-17, NIVB*

Truly this is the "Great Mystery of Our God," the Great I Am ! This is "the Way of Holiness!"

Recently the Lord spoke to me and so graciously gave me a vision..Oh, His kindness to me is so undeserved yet I rejoice in Him and His love! I was praying in the Spirit on January 23, 2018, the Lord opened my eyes and ears to hear.

"There has never been such a great of movement of the Holy Spirit over all mankind as is now beginning. Not only from your east to west coasts but all around the world. Everything will seem in chaos but the end will be order and joy and thanksgiving," said the Lord to me.

As in an earlier vision, I see in vision again people in the streets dancing and rejoicing and praising God! The news media will not be able to keep up with all the changes taking place around the globe. The Holy Spirit I see is breaking out everywhere. breaking down barriers between people (not one world government order but one world freed from sin and darkness. One world under God, our Heavenly Jesus!) (I prayed again in the spirit tongues)

I see people saying "Look! I am young again! Is this the God we have despised and forsaken? Is this the God we hated? I gave Him anguish and He has given goodness and Mercy. He has given me beauty for the ashes I offered to Him, love for my hate,He has given me the breath of life in exchange for the breath of death and darkness! Has there ever been such a God as this!" end of vision.

Then He ended with this short message. "To all those who love Me, keep up the walk of Faith, believe in Me your Savior Jesus. All will be as it should be!"

" Father, because you will it!" I answered" I surrender my will to your will!"

Oh, *Magnificence and Depth* is our God!

19 REVELATION-THE MIND OF CHRIST

One night I was playing the guitar and singing. I stopped and said, "Lord, I want to sing a song just for you!" He quickly gave me the words below-words which after examining them appeared to be a prophetic message. Later, I realized they were supposed to be given to a particular worship group. But in retrospect, it is very apt for those who love the Lord. These are the words to the song:

HE IS OUR KING!

Yes, He was a Carpenter. Yes, He is our King!

He wears no earthly garments; He is not of this world. No, He is not of this world.

He wears a robe of righteousness. Glory is His to own. Yes, His Father's Glory is His to own.

Look not to the world for guidance. Put your trust in Him

today, and live, live in Him.

Come out of the shadows of Babylon. Cast those shackles away. Be free, free in Him.

You are His people, He made you. How can you turn Him away? Choose...choose Him!

There is no sorrow where He is; He takes care of His own. So smile, smile for Him.

Yes, He was a carpenter. Yes, He is our King!

> A message followed the song:
> Thus speaks the Lord unto you: Fear not, for I shall not leave you homeless or without food or drink; for you shall surely drink from the vineyards of My Father. He who hath Me, hath the Father.
> Do not trust in those things of the world which must corrode and rot, but rather seek after those things which are life giving and of value: virtue, tolerance, and brotherly kindness.
> I walk not in crooked paths. I set a judgment and it is done.
> [*Note: At this point I saw the Lord with power coming forth from His mouth. There was no time element between that which He spoke and that which was fulfilled.*]
> My Mouth speaks forth power and the elements obey! Prepare now for the storm that is coming. Wait not until the shutters rattle at your windows.
> Then I heard parts of a familiar hymn. Following that, I heard a loud voice declare: This is the age of My Glory! This is the age of My Victory. Amen.

Jesus loves to communicate with His children. He loves to be part of every conversation that we have with others. I have noticed that when I am speaking to someone on the phone about spiritual things, He will join in the conversation. He adds many meaty and enlightening truths to the conversation.

He has spoken many times through Jerry and me and continues to speak fluently and prophetically through me. What a blessing the Spirit of Truth is! This is a gift that He wants all of His children to activate in their life! If we have been born again or baptized with the Holy Ghost, we already have it!

"But the Comforter, which is the Holy Ghost, whom the Father will send in My name, He shall teach you all things..." ~*John 14:26, KJV*

Mundane household chores are always peppered with spicy conversations with the Lord. He teaches us constantly. For example, I was scrubbing our shower stall and visiting with Him about rewards one day.

As a youngster I read about Dr. Albert Schweitzer. He became a hero of mine. He was the most remarkable man I had ever read about, short of Jesus. He gave up a famous music career to become a missionary physician. He left behind everything of the world, moved to Africa, and established a hospital there.

I was visiting with Jesus, saying how Dr. Schweitzer should receive a reward much greater than many of us, as he had dedicated so much of his life for others. Then Jesus said a stunning thing! He said it so simply:

"I Am your reward."

I was flabbergasted! Weren't people who died given rewards on different levels according to their works? I never thought of Jesus as being THE REWARD; I thought He was the reward-er! My religious tradition of the past laid as broken pieces at my feet! What a shock! Reality began to manifest itself.

"He that hath seen Me hath seen the Father...I Am in the Father, and the Father in me..." ~*John 14:9-10, KJV*

Excitement bubbled up in me!

"And unto all riches of the full assurance of understanding, to the acknowledgment of the mystery of God, and of the Father, and of Christ: in Whom are hid all the treasures of wisdom and knowledge." ~*Colossians 2:2-3, KJV*

"All the treasures of wisdom and knowledge." They are mine?

"For in Him dwelleth all the fullness of the Godhead bodily. And ye are complete in Him, which is the head of all principality and power ." ~*Colossians 2:9-10, KJV*

"In Him dwelleth all the fullness of the Godhead bodily." Me too?

The parable of the laborers now makes perfect sense. The ones who worked all day got the same reward as the ones who only worked an hour; their reward was Jesus! (Matt. 20:1-15)

"For in Him we live, and move and have our being...For we are also His offspring." ~*Acts 17:28, KJV*

He is in the Father and the Father in Him, and They will come and sup within us!

Jesus is Eternity! So therefore, we are in Eternity and Eternity is in us! He is our reward!

Hallelujah!

Later, Christ reminded me how His apostles argued over which one of them would be the greatest in the kingdom of God. He said to them: "Ye know that the princes of the Gentiles exercise dominion over them, and they that are great exercise authority upon them. But it shall not be so among you: but whosoever will be great among you, let him be your minister; and whosoever will be chief among you, let him be your servant. Even the Son of man came not to be ministered unto, but to minister, and to give His life a ransom for many." ~*Matthew 20:25-28, KJV*

Christ continued teaching me saying, "Man thinks in terms of horizontal levels: 'This level is higher than this one.'" (Like I was thinking Dr. Schweitzer was higher.) But in reality, Jesus explained, He Himself is like the Sun and our paths run vertically like the sun's rays. Each of us comes ever and always closer to Him in our understanding as the Holy Ghost teaches us. His Spirit intertwined with our spirit is ever perfect in us, but our carnal mind needs to be renewed like our spirit. Again, Christ does the works in us; our part is receiving these revelations of truth that He gives us.

"But unto you that fear My name shall the Sun of righteousness arise with healing in His wings..." ~*Malachi 4:2, KJV*

The gift of prophecy-revelation has become a thing of the past for too many church organizations. Some church organizations are fortunate to have one or two prophetic words a month. Some are dried up because they think that Jesus quit speaking to people 2000 years ago! There are some which replace the Holy Ghost with "enthusiasm," or "intellectualism" (man's/world's wisdom). Their congregations are like tombs filled with dead men bones!

"Having a form of godliness, but denying the power thereof..." ~*2 Timothy 3:5, KJV*

The Holy Spirit is what gives churches life and joy!

More churches today though are turning to the gifts of the Holy Spirit and are becoming alive again! However, I think we misunderstand the prophetic word! Although prophecy does tell about future events, it does more than that. Prophecy is actually what is meant by "Having the mind of Christ, the Holy Spirit." When we are baptized with fire, our spirit mind is renewed and restored to Jesus and to His direction. Jesus is revealed through the Holy Ghost.

"For the testimony of Jesus is the Spirit of prophecy." ~*Revelations 19:10, KJV*

I have heard that the mind of our spirit man is our spiritual heart! "And He that searcheth the hearts knoweth what is the mind of the Spirit..." ~*Romans 8:27, KJV* If that is true, the first thing we must do is to make our heart ready so that it can be plowed and prepared by Holy Spirit to receive God's Words. Jesus told me that "faith" comes by listening to His voice personally every day!

"For God, who commanded the light to shine out of darkness, has shined in our hearts, to give the light of the knowledge of the glory of God in the face of Jesus Christ. But we have this treasure (Jesus in us) in earthen vessels (our physical bodies), that the excellency of the power may be of God and not of us!" ~*2 Corinthians 4:6, KJV,* inserts mine

Our tongues are very powerful, as mentioned in an earlier chapter. Let them be used for sharing the revelations of the Lord with others! Let us enjoy having the "mind of Christ," for we are all one in Him, as shown by our love for each other.

Hallelujah! All of Himself and His love is our great reward! He is our great Reward!

One morning I was looking for something in the

scriptures when the Lord spoke to me saying sadly:

"They have forgotten their God!" Clarifying, He said, "They have forgotten that I love them!" (They- meaning His people.)

Then He added: "They have forgotten that I love them! They are wandering around like homeless kittens seeking what they do not know; howling in the night with pain, agony, and despair! They have forgotten, or they have not known the love I have for them!"

"Tell them quickly, My daughter! Tell them, for of such is the kingdom prepared for!"

The Heavenly Father pleads, "Come to Me, My little lost ones, and I will give you peace! I will hold you in my arms and lift you up and smile and say, "You are my beloved, little ones!" I will lift you up and you shall see the wonders of Your God! Be comforted; your heavenly Father loves only you! Come, come to Me!"

Another morning I woke up to an open vision like a movie production. The sound was so loud and the dust was stirred up and billowed upward around me. I quickly recognized through the dust clouds that I was flanking a flock of stampeding sheep. There were so many I could not see the beginning, end, nor the depth of the flock. The whole experience was so real! I asked the Lord, over the sounds of the stampeding sheep ,"Lord, what does this mean?"

The vision of the sheep passed as quickly as it had come.

He replied in His familiar voice, "My sheep are running away because they are frightened of Me. They don't know how much I love them."

I asked, "Why?" I could not imagine anyone being afraid of My Wonderful God.

The Lord then explained to me that man has been

taught by the precepts of men that He is a mean, vengeful, and wrathful God always wanting to condemn them, punish them, and anxious to send them to hell. Again I could hear the disappointment in Father God's voice!

At another time Jesus spoke to me about this subject.

"There were people who loved and cared for Me when I walked the earth. They wanted Me near to them. But even some of the prophets thought that I was severe at times. This is reflected in some of their writings. Take Jeremiah for instance. They saw Me though the veil of their eyes , just as you do today."

"Some see Me as the conquering hero."

I have a short vision here. The Lord is carrying the Word as a sword. Thousands are converted and taken into God's Kingdom.

"It is by My mighty hand that you will accomplish your purposes. My hand is not slack that I cannot recover all that *seems* lost!"

"Oh, my child, I so desire to comfort you! Let My light flow through you and you will continue to see Me. Do you think that others wonder how you can be content with just Me by your side. Even you are amazed! I was more a part of you than you imagined."(Referring to time after Jerry's passing.)

"Did I not tell you, if you just believed, your words would change nations. There is no distance to My Spirit. You can pray right now for a nation like Canada."

"Be what I have called you to be, a vessel filled with My Flaming Fire!"

"Lord Jesus of Nazareth," I answered. "You are and have always been my Flaming Fire! Even my Spirit of Truth. Amen.

20 WHAT HAPPENED IN PARADISE?

"Wherefore, as by one man sin entered into the world, and death by sin; and so death passed upon all men for that all have sinned." ~*Romans. 5:12, KJV*

"Nevertheless, death reigned from Adam to Moses, even over them that had not sinned after the similitude of Adam's transgression... *Romans 5:14 KJV*

Our eyes can become very glazed over, not comprehending the darkness of this world. Some of us get accustomed to the morals of the day and do not recognize what is happening. I have been in that mindset before. However, the Lord opens our eyes and our ears by His love and His loveliness! We look forward to Jesus being King Messiah ruling over the earth. Earth will then be Paradise again! He is waiting on us. "

"For if by one man's offense death reigned by one; much more they which receive abundance of grace and of the gift of righteousness shall reign in life by one, Jesus Christ. Therefore as by the offense of one judgment came upon all men to condemnation; even so by the righteousness of one the free gift came upon all men unto justification of life. For as by one man's disobedience many were made sinners, so by the obedience of one shall many be made righteous." ~*Romans 5:17-19, KJV*

As I mentioned in a previous chapter, Adam and Eve must have been devastated by the death of Able when he was murdered by their other son, Cain. They had never seen death before—ever!

We raise horses. If a mare's baby dies, she does not understand death! She will pull at the baby's ears to lift the head to try to get some response. The mare will stand around for hours sometimes, and then finally she will turn away in sorrow and walk away! Then we bury the foal. I am not comparing a human life with a horse, though it is a tragedy for them as well as people! But this story is an example of how it was with Adam and Eve.

Death is "barrenness!"

What happened in Paradise?

The Lord spoke to me about the Tree of Knowledge of Good and Evil from which Adam and Eve ate. He showed me how most of us focus on the good and the evil of the tree instead of the word *Knowledge*.

I had always thought that Adam and Eve, by eating from the tree of good and evil, gave us our agency to choose between good and evil. But I had missed the whole picture! Adam and Eve had free agency before they ate of the tree! God wanted His children to enjoy all the blessings of Paradise. He allowed that corrupting tree to be in Paradise so Adam and Eve could choose whether to listen to and obey their heavenly Father's counsel or not. There is no freedom where there is no choice. There is no love where there is no freedom.

I had also thought, their eating from the tree of knowledge was what allowed them to have children. But again sexual intimacy is not what the tree gave them, for the Lord had commanded Adam and Eve to "multiply and replenish the earth" before the serpent came along to tempt them. I had associated carnal knowledge only with sexual knowledge and activities, which is incorrect!

Jesus pointed out to me that I needed to focus on the knowledge part of the tree, for it represents carnal knowledge—the intellectual wisdom of the world/our carnal mind! It is man's worship of his own thinking and opinions (idolatry)! And out of this worldly wisdom comes our love of judging everyone and everything by our own measure of rightness- what we ourselves believe is right thinking and right doing. Out of the knowledge of good and evil came *the law*.

"When the woman saw that the fruit of the tree was good for food and pleasing to the eye, and also desirable for gaining wisdom (the wisdom of the world), she took some and ate it!" ~*Genesis 3:6, NIV*, insert mine

The Lord brought me more words on this subject much later. He said,"Never before in history have I longed more than I do now that My Earth would be restored to it's former magnificance. When I first created it for man. Everything was aglow with my light and My love! It still amazes Me, that they could think that there was something better that they were missing out on. "

"Lord," I answered. "I understand what you mean. Our horses will be grazing on 30 acres of land , yet will stick their nose through the fence and grab grass on the other side."

The Lord continued, "They actually believed the lie of satan, that I was holding out on them because I did not want them to eat of the tree which would cause the destruction of them and their generations following. I had to put the tree of the world's wisdom there so they would have free agency."

In a revelation given to Mitt Jeffords. He was shown that the greatest lust of man is *"to be right."* When I read this, I knew it was literally true. I knew because I stood as a prime example. All I had to do was go look in a mirror and say, "Zap, Vivien, I gotcha!" *"To be right"* is the greatest lust of the carnal mind/flesh. I was completely flabbergasted because anything so simple and true is not commonly known or spoken of. Why has this never been revealed or preached about before?

I remembered how the Lord hates *self-right-ness,* or shall we call it the *know it all* judgments we burden others with! I am sorry to admit that most people, including myself, at some time in their life have felt superior because they knew the right way to believe and act, (religious spirit.) Jesus had to come and save us from *our self*. He has been working decades molding me saving me from *me, myself and I, the carnal mind*. Remember what the serpent told Eve: "If you eat of this you will be as gods, knowing...! *Self* will reign supreme!" Believing in *Self* is what we need to repent of.

Being *the expert* or *knowing it all* is the opposite of humility. Humility is not feeling unworthy, worthless, or like a failure. Humility is recognizing that each one of us is an equally valuable child of God and that we desire God's wisdom, not our own. Humility is being teachable. Sometimes our mouths are flapping and we are not listening to the Holy Spirit or others whom God has taught. If so, we may need to pray for deliverance from this. Here is a simple prayer that could be said:

"Forgive me, Lord. Please cast out that lustful spirit of I know. Deliver me, please, from desiring to be my own god, *me, myself and I,* for only You can be God. Thank you that this sin has already been covered by Your blood! In Jesus name...Amen."

"Two men went up to the temple to pray, one a Pharisee and the other a tax collector. The Pharisee stood and prayed thus with himself. ' God, I thank You that I am not like other men-extortioners, unjust, adulterers, or even as this tax collector.' And the tax collector , standing afar off, would not so much as raise his eyes to heaven, but beat his breast, saying,'God, be merciful to me a sinner!' I tell you, this man went down to his house justified rather than the other, for everyone who exalts himself will be humbled, and he who humbles himself will be exalted." *~Luke 18:10-14 NKJV*

Now relate the above scripture to this scripture: "Many will say to Me in that day, 'Lord, Lord, have *we* not prophesied in Your name,(*we*) cast out demons in Your name, and (*we*)done many wonders in Your name?' And then I will declare to them ,'I never knew you, depart from Me, you who practice lawlessness!" ~*Matthew 7:21-23* inserts mine.

It all came together suddenly as to why Jesus spoke to the high priests and the elders of the Temple, saying: "Verily I say unto you, that the publicans and the harlots will go into the kingdom of God before you." ~*Matthew 21:31, KJV*

The publicans and harlots believed and followed Jesus! The high priests and elders chose their own legalism/law and intellectualism over *Jesus, The Word*!

When we eat from the *I am right* intellectualism tree, our hearts are hardened against the Spirit of Truth! And a hardened heart is a dark and difficult place for the full love of God to reside! Many religions are based on man's knowledge of the scripture-what man himself reasons out from his human understanding or precepts is good and evil/the law.

The TREE OF KNOWLEDGE is man's pride in:

His intellect,

His own reasoning,

His own mind,

His own "brilliance," and

His own opinions of what is right! (the law)

Adam and Eve chose the tree of carnal knowledge, *their own reasoning/law*. They listened to *the worlds wisdom* given through Satan rather than *God's Wisdom*. Because of this, death came upon all their children, including us!

Darkness results when we choose our own intellectual thinking rather than Jesus' understanding! The more we go from the Garden of Paradise(Eden) into man's world and worldly thinking, the more we move into darkness! The more we go from worldly thinking to "The Tree of Life" (God's thoughts and understanding) the more we move into light!

We drink from the fountain of Living Water and eat from the Tree of Life when we study the Word of God under the tutelage of the Holy Ghost. When we pick up the scripture and study with our own minds to reason it out, we are eating of the tree of worldly wisdom.

The Lord revealed to me that the cross that Jesus was nailed to was in fact the tree of knowledge of good and evil ie the law ie the curse. It was the world's wisdom and world's judgment on mankind:"death!" But through Christ's physical death and resurrection He secured victory for us over the devil: the devil's works-sin, and death. The tree of knowledge and death was transformed by His blood into the Tree of Life! His judgment on mankind was "life." "Father forgive them for they know not what they do!" ~Luke 23:34

Jesus reigns supreme because He is supreme! There is no teacher like Him! The Tree of Life represents Jesus in every way. He is indeed the Tree of Life itself! When we eat of Him and allow Him to be the reasoning in our hearts, exchanging ur thoughts for His thoughts and allowing His mind to be ours, then we will be filled with His light, His life, and His love! What can He not do through His children who choose to be His hands, mouth, and feet?

"As the living Father hath sent Me (Jesus), and I live by the Father: so he that eateth Me, even he shall live by Me." ~John 6:57, KJV, insert is mine

The Spirit of Truth resides in our spirit not in our intellect. Christ says He judges the intent of the heart. The heart is the part which He is concerned about!

"For they that are after the flesh do mind the things of the flesh; but they that are after the Spirit, the things of the Spirit. For to be carnally minded is death; but to be spiritually minded is life and peace. Because the carnal mind is enmity against God; for it is not subject to the law of

God (The Law of Love), neither indeed can be. So they that are in the "flesh" cannot please God." ~*Romans 8:5-8, KJV*, insert by me

Jesus said,"Marvel not that I said unto thee, ye must be born again. The wind bloweth where it listeth, and thou hearest the sound thereof, but canst not tell whence it cometh, and whither it goeth: so is every one that is born of the Spirit." ~*John 3:7-8, KJV*

My understanding of the vision that I shared in chapter 17 continues to grow! *I will repeat that vision here for your convenience and relate it to Adam and Eve and their Garden experience.*

"One day I was visiting with Jesus. I found myself in an open vision. I was standing looking out on a flat, barren desert. I could see miles of dry parched land in all directions. I saw a wrought iron chair sitting there in front and to the left of me. When I walked around it and sat down, the Lord told me that 'my sitting down' represented 'my resting in Him.' The minute I sat down, fountains of Living Water broke forth all over that wasteland! Streams and rivers were formed, and it was beautiful and wonderful to behold." I have just received another analogy from it.

The prose and poetry of the Lord's language written in His word, contains a language pattern called chiasm. A chiasm is when the Lord speaks something and then repeats the same ideas in the reverse sequence, with the most important idea usually being in the middle. It is meant to emphasize a Word He wants you to pay attention to.

For an example, I'll use *Matthew 11:28-30 NIVB*:

1. Come to Me, all you who are weary and burdened,

2. and I will give you rest. Take My yoke upon you

3. and learn from Me, for I am gentle and humble in heart,

2. and you will find rest for your souls. For My yoke is easy

1. and My burden is light.

As you can see, the two 1's are similar, as are the two 2's. The most important thought is in line 3.

Look up chiasms in the Bible or on the web. They are fascinating! I created a chiasm based on my vision and the story of Adam and Eve. Here it is:

Adam and Eve lived in the perfect Paradise. Rivers of Living Water were running everywhere. ~*Genesis 2:10-14, KJV* Then they stood at the tree and picked the fruit of "*the world's wisdom and knowledge.*" Suddenly they looked around and Paradise had become a barren desert!

On the other hand, my vision is the perfect picture of someone sitting on the "Mercy Seat of Grace." I looked around and everything was barren and dead. Then I sat down on the mercy seat of "Christ's finished work-Grace." Everything became alive!

1. Adam and Eve (Created in God's image)

  2. Lived in the Paradise of God

    3. Man stood and picked the fruit (self performance/the law)

      4. Fruit = worldly wisdom and knowledge

      5. Death = Barren desert to man

        6. Christ (A New Adam) came and changed man's destiny

      5. Death = Barren desert restored to grace /replaced law

      4. Fruit = God's wisdom, love, peace, and joy

    3. Believers sit down on Mercy Seat (Jesus' finished work)

2. Now living in perfection of God

1. Transformed man (Jesus is birthed in the believer — spiritually created in God's image. His mind in us.)

Hallelujah!

"For if through the offense of one many be dead, much more the grace of God, and the gift of grace, which is by one man, Jesus Christ, hath abounded unto many."~*Romans 5:12 KJV*

21 A SUITCASE LABELED "FEAR"

"Peace I leave with you, My peace I give unto you: not as the world gives, give I unto you. Let not your heart be troubled, neither let it be afraid." ~*John 14:27, KJV*

Why does the Lord tell us so often not to be afraid? There are at least 42 places in His Word, where He says, "Fear not!"

Fear is not an emotion. It is an entity, a spirit. It is one of the greatest weapons in the arsenal of the devil that he uses against all of us! Especially if we are God's children!

The Lord told me to look at fear as if it were a suitcase. You would never choose to pick up a suitcase that did not belong to you at an airport. Neither should you choose to allow fear to enter your mind and heart. Fear does not belong to the children of the Most High God! So if you find a suitcase labeled "fear," let it stay on the conveyor belt headed for the pit! It does not, nor ever will, belong to you!

Fear is an enemy to God. Fear comes with the spirit of dread. They are both enemies to God's purposes for man. They keep man from coming to God! They are of darkness. Fear is opposite of love!

Fear prophesies doom and gloom into our lives! And when we speak fearful prophecies, they become reality in our minds! The one thing that we fear and dread the most, if we constantly dwell on it, will probably happen in our life. We bring darkness to ourselves and to others by speaking words of fear and dread!

These spirits of fear and dread are planted in our hearts and mind by Satan! They are sometimes delivered to us by other people as well! If someone is prophesying only doom and gloom, I politely walk away. God does not give us the spirits of fear or dread!

"For God hath not given us the spirit of fear; but of power, and of love, and of a sound mind." ~*2 Timothy 1:7, KJV*

Compelling people to become righteous by performance through man's doctrine or the world's wisdom rather than the righteousness and love of Jesus is promoting fear!

God says, "Foreamuch as this people draw near Me with their mouth, and with their lips do honor Me, but have removed their heart far from Me, and their fear toward Me is taught by the precept of men." ~*Isaiah 29:13 KJV*

How does the devil plant fear in our hearts?

Think on this: Would you listen to someone if you knew he was a liar? What if he had a charismatic personality, would you then believe him? Would you believe someone who told you the things you wanted to hear? The devil even uses men to proclaim his abominations! What if the devil used your own mind to proclaim his lies to you by your own thoughts! Would you believe the lies?

Jesus speaking of the devil says this: "He was a murderer from the beginning, and abode not in the truth, because there is no truth in him, When he peaketh a lie, he speaketh of his own: for he is a liar, and the father of it." ~*John 8:44 KJV*

He is definitely a murderer because his lies can be devastating! Look how he brought Adam and Eve and all of mankind to death by his lies! Fear has brought many to suicide! How tragic it is when fear literally scares some people to death! They do not know that what they are thinking *is not their own thoughts;* it is the spirit of fear and dread overtaking them!

The wicked one is very subtle. I can sympathize with Eve a little because of his sly ways. Satan knows each of our personal speaking patterns and the words we use! Our speaking patterns are just like our thought patterns. *He can plant his thoughts into our minds, making them sound exactly like our own voice and cause us to believe they are our own.* But in fact they are his lies! I discovered this extremely important information one evening.

I had heard that our granddaughter was going in for tests for a spot on her skin. All of a sudden, I started getting these horrendous, scary thoughts, and began to be fearful. Then I realized that those thoughts, were not the way I think anymore. I have grown to trust God so much, that there is very little fear in my heart today.

So I said, "In the name of Jesus, these are not my thoughts, Satan, but they are thoughts you are planting in my mind! Get out of here!"

Immediately the spirit of fear left, and I was full of faith in the Lord's goodness, believing that everything was going to be just fine for my granddaughter. And it was!

"Fear hath torment." *~1 John 4:18, KJV* Basking in God's love is Glory!

Fear certainly does have torment! Just think of some of the fears Satan puts in our heart! We fear losing our loved ones, our health, our necessities, our job, our possessions, our positions of honor and titles, our life, our salvation, and the list goes on and on! All of us as humans can relate to this! The spirit of fear lies to mankind about God! Fear can even tell us that God could never love us because of how bad we are!

"As haunting as these groups of fear were, it was the next group of haunting spirits that really frightened me. These were the spirits whose only nature and purpose for being was to try and haunt us in our relationship, our communion, and our fellowship with God." (Mitt Jeffords' writing, Chapter 4)

There are unclean spirits as well. "These unclean spirits were named envy, malice, rage, depression, jealousy, unforgiveness, confusion, frustration, contention, bitterness, covetousness, vengefulness, strife, hatred, lusts, and anger." (Mitt Jeffords' writing, Chapter 4)

"It was here that for the first time I began to understand why the Lord says that death rules over the thoughts of the carnal mind. Up until this time, I just thought the death of the carnal mind only had to do with man's "separation from God," but I now see that the very nature of these troubling, and miserable, and tormenting thoughts was death itself." (Mitt Jeffords' writing, Chapter 4)

Can we see that all this torment is caused by the spirits which Satan plants in our mind? God has the answer and the answer is in the power of the name of Jesus! In His name we can cast them out!

"For this purpose the Son of God was manifested, that He might destroy the works of the devil." *~1 John 3:8, KJV*

If it seems like I keep repeating this truism, I am! Because it must be set firmly in our minds that Jesus has set us free of these detestable things! He has already broken the chains that have bound us and still bind us! We are free; however, do we know that we are free? This reminds me of a story I once heard second or third handed. It was many years ago. It was a lengthy story inspired by the Holy Spirit. However, I will sum it all up quickly in a few paragraphs:

A man had two beautiful eagles which he doted on continuously. Nothing was too good for them! Their feathers were shiny and their eyes bright with health. They even looked as if they were always smiling-if eagles can smile.B ut one day while the owner was away on business, a wicked man came and kidnapped them. He thrust their big bodies into a small filthy cage. He treated them meanly, feeding them measly crumbs and water.

The owner of the eagles wept when he arrived back home and found his eagles gone. He could not find them. Finally after searching for them and hiring others to search for them, the eagles were located. Much to the owner's chagrin, the wicked man who stole them asked an unbelievable ransom for them. So high was the ransom that the bird owner would have to sell everything he owned to pay. But to the owner of the birds, nothing was too much to give for their return. He reminisced about their sitting on his shoulder or arm and their soaring high above the mountains. Always they returned to him with a beak to mouth kiss!

"No, nothing," he determined in his heart; then speaking out loud he said: "Nothing is too much to give for them!"

The owner paid the ransom. He anticipated holding his birds in his arms again. Anger arose in him when he looked into the cage and saw their condition. They were dirty, thin, and scraggly, but they were still alive! That was most important to him. He opened the cage and called them by name. One eagle immediately hopped out of the cage and jumped onto his shoulder, but the other remained inside! No amount of coaxing could bring the second eagle out of the cage. There was no explanation for it! Had the second eagle forgotten the happiness he had experienced with his owner and rescuer? Did he feel comfortable within the bondage and abuse he was receiving from the kidnapper? No one knows!

My ending of the story would be that the owner destroys the evil man and his wickedness. He begins working with the second eagle until he is restored. Only those experiencing and living in bondage can end this story for themselves.

Like the second eagle, do we know we are now free? Are we filled with joy because our owner has saved us from our kidnappers-even the spirits of fear and dread! Or are we trapped within? Jesus will come into our hearts if we only ask Him to. He will by the fan andthe fire destroy all of our enemies, if we are willing. Simply ask!

There are many concepts which the Lord opens our eyes to see. For example, it mentions in the scriptures that Satan can appear as an Angel of Light, *~2 Corinthians 11:14*

He certainly can and has done so. However, the Holy Spirit gives us discernment between good and evil. Nevertheless, if there is any question, we need only to ask that spirit if it will confess that Jesus has come in the flesh, was born of a virgin, crucified for our sins, buried, rose from the dead, and lives forever more! If it is an evil spirit, it will never agree with this!

A few years ago I had a "spirit" literally come to me and entice me to take him in. I simply said, "No! The only spirit I have anything to do with is Jesus!" Of course, he left instantly and never bothered me again!

We have dominion over the spirits of evil! This is one of the victories Jesus won for us. He told His disciples the following words, even though they had not yet received the baptism of the Holy Ghost:

"Behold, I give unto you power to tread on serpents and scorpions, and over all the power of the enemy, and nothing shall by any means hurt you."~*Luke 10:18-19; KJV*

One Thursday while doing our prayer rounds at the hospital, we entered a room and asked the woman patient if she would like us to pray for her. She quickly responded, "Yes!" She apologized because one time earlier in the year she had abruptly sent us away from her room saying she was mad at God. However, this time she said she would really appreciate prayers.

I was very happy she had allowed us to do so, for I saw three dark entities standing by her bed. They were a dark putrid gray color and looked identical. Our recent Holy Ghost training gave us confidence. I stepped right into their space and they fled. We called on the power of the Holy Spirit to bless this woman. Later the Lord revealed to me that those evil entities were strongholds in this woman's life, and now they had been defeated by His power.

If a thought is negative or accusatory, instead a loving, corrective word in due season, know that it is not the Lord speaking to you or through you! When Jesus corrects us, He corrects us with love! He does not tell us how unworthy or terrible we are! So when accusatory thoughts attack us, we need to "take every thought of Satan captive" and kick him out! Oh, the wondrous authority we have in the name of Jesus!

"Now the serpent was more subtle than any beast of the field which the Lord God had made." ~*Genesis 3:1; KJV*

One spring night before retiring to bed, an impression of a snake began to intrude upon my mind. I had no idea why a snake would be bothering my mind. I hate snakes so I avoid thinking of them! About 1:30 in the morning, I woke up alert. And in my mind's eye, I saw a vision of a shiny, black serpent. He raised himself up in front of me and kept preening himself. His beady eyes were full of pride! Oh, he was showing himself off saying, "Look at how beautiful I am!"

I saw more pride than I had ever seen in a human being! Because I did not want to wake Jerry up by speaking out-loud, I kept saying in my thoughts to the snake, "I do not want you bothering me!" I do not believe Satan cannot hear our thoughts. I went quietly into another room and the vision remained.

"Oh, look how beautiful I am!" He continued. Surprisingly, he did not frighten me, but it was just extremely unpleasant! Before I returned to bed, I said out-loud abruptly to him: "Take it up with Jesus; He's the authority over me!"

Immediately he was gone, and I felt such a relief from the pressure of the serpent's presence. I started praising the Lord for being such a wonderful Savior to save me from such an experience as this. I started singing praise songs to Jesus in my heart! Then I asked the Lord what this experience was all about, for the serpent had nothing that I desired.

The Lord said, "Satan desires to entice all of the Father's children into worshiping him, especially those who are committed to the Heavenly Father. Satan worships himself and believes his own lies so much that he expects everyone to be as impressed as he is with himself. He is angry with any form of worship and glory given to Me, the

Father in Heaven, especially by My Children."

The Lord also said that Jerry and I were shaking up Satan's kingdom because we were going in the authority of Jesus' name, not of our own. He told me that He give Jerry and me His wisdom on any matter if we would simply ask! This experience confirmed the truth to me that those "born of the Spirit" have power to tread on and dispel serpents through Jesus name!

"And He said unto them, I beheld Satan as lightning fall from heaven. Behold, I give unto you power to tread on serpents and scorpions, and over all the power of the enemy and nothing shall by any means hurt you." ~*Luke 10:18-19, KJV*

After the serpent fled my vision, and after praising the Lord, I adjured the Lord to pour out Living Water on me so I could enjoy His presence for a while, which He did, and I was able to go back to sleep. Praise God! In a dream that directly followed, Jerry and I were in a very beautiful, architectural garden where there were pillars with arches. While we rested there, we were being rained on by Living Water!

Hallelujah!

"As the living Father hath sent Me (Jesus), and I live by the Father: so he that eateth Me, even he shall live by Me." ~*John 6:57, KJV,* insert is mine

"We did not take the spirit of the world but the Spirit which is from God, so that we would know the things freely given to us by God!" ~*1 Corinthians.2:12, NMB*

When I feel fear heading toward me, I repeat this verse: "There is no fear in love; but perfect love casteth out fear." ~*1 John 4:18, KJV*

Fear can be defeated! You can start by recognizing it. Fear and dread are spirits; therefore they can be cast out in the name of Jesus! If this does not work for you, ask for the Holy Spirit to come in and take this fear and dread away. Know that He will do it if we are willing to believe. Jesus loves doing this work! As I said in an earlier chapter, it is easy for Him. He does not want any of us to live a fearful life, instead He wants us to be filled with the joy, the peace, and the security of His love for us!

"But the fruit of the Spirit is love, joy, peace, long suffering, gentleness, goodness, faith." ~*Galatians 5:22, KJV*

One day I was writing in my journal. "Lord, I will sing praises unto You! For You are the most high God! I pray that all idols be cast down and only the Name of the Lord be praised and only He be worshipped. Lord I am very concerned over many things in this world. Yet, I know that You are the answer to every concern that I have. Therefore, I lay all these concerns at your feet!

The Lord answered "...Let not your heart be troubled over anything in your life. I have established earth as a footstool so that my foot, the places that I tread, may rest there. Has it not been said *wherever you tread will be yours*. Well, wherever I rest My feet I claim as Mine! So be not afraid or discouraged about the state of affairs of this world, for I walk over all the earth, and My eyes search for those who seek Me and cry out. My eyes also search with loving kindness those that need My succor. For I am always there for those who love Me, I am their constant companion. Their truth, their life! Surely Goodness and Mercy do follow them and they do dwell In My house and shall do forever! ...Take no thought for what you shall eat or drink or wear for I am with you. My strong right Arm will comfort you and lift you up. All things are as they should be in your life..." Amen.

22 CHOOSE LIFE OR DEATH

My Husband gave a word from the Lord to our in-home worship group about the separation between good and evil becoming much greater in the world. All people will have to make a choice: to choose light or darkness.

This word was so simple, yet so powerful that it just went to my heart and became like a drumbeat. Light or darkness! Life or death! I began to line up the things of light and the things of darkness in my mind. It proved very enlightening.

Love, compassion, peace, joy, life, and more of the same are the light side. "But the fruit of the Spirit is love, joy, peace, longsuffering, gentleness, goodness, faith, meekness, temperance: against such there is no law." ~*Galatians 5:22-23, KJV*

Disease? Wow, it definitely was on the dark side! Worry, discouragement, and fear? They also are on the dark side, etc. Make a list yourself. It is extremely helpful!

Early the next morning, I awoke from a sound sleep. I sat up in bed, and in a vision I saw my body lying out before me in mid air. The Lord spoke and said, "Do you choose life or death?"

I was not afraid, for I knew the Lord's voice and knew He was still instructing me. He had been teaching me the previous day about what things line up with either darkness or light. At that moment, the Lord revealed to me the grave importance of choosing life or death. The moment I looked at my body, I could feel the power of life and death! I of course said "Life!" I pray to my God and Savior that all men will want to choose Jesus, for in Him does all life reside!

Never a boring moment with Jesus of Nazereth!

Choosing to speak life, not death, is extremely important. Our words have unbelievable power! They too are like a two-edged sword that can cut into other people's hearts and wound them. I have done that a number of times and have hurt those who are dear to me! You can be forgiven, but the wound remains for years sometimes. Let us choose life not death-positive blessings, not negative cursing!

Like God's words, our words will not return to us void-whether for life or for death, light or darkness. Let us send forth light into the universe and into the lives of our loved ones!

Proverbs 18:21 says,"Death and life are in the power of the tongue: and they that love it shall eat the fruit thereof."

One day, I thought it would be fun to answer all my immediate family telephone calls with a silly answer. They would say, "How are you doing?" I would answer "Oh, just hanging out like bats!"

On the second day of answering a few calls that way, and while working at my computer, a black, flying object came toward me. It was literally diving and darting. I started running and screaming! "Jerry, help! There is a bat in here."

In one horrifying moment, I became a believer in the power of words! No more mentioning bats or any other terrible thing that could manifest in the flesh! I was convinced!

Words can cause the most powerful blessings or curses! Diseases can manifest in our bodies by our words. Many people have been healed by decreeing God's promises of healing. There are many lists of healing promises on the internet that we have access to. We need to print them off of our computers and hang them in places where we can look at them often. Also it is great to share these printed copies with those who are ill.

Satan regularly interjects thoughts of illness in our minds. We begin to believe his lies. If we look in the mirror, he suggests that we look tired, and we start to feel weary in a minute! It is all about what we believe and who we believe in.

How was the universe created? God's Word! Our faith shows forth when we believe that the universes were made by God speaking a word. Faith is believing there is no time between His speaking a word and it being manifested. God knows anything is possible, God is Faith. Heaven knows anything is possible because they know God. When we are born again, we are given the Spirit of Christ! We are given His faith which knows that all things are possible. We are as Christ is in this world! If we believed all things were possible, we could indeed move mountains by merely speaking a word!

"Herein is our love made perfect, that we may have boldness in the day of judgment: because as He is, so are we in this world." ~*1 John 4:17, KJV*

So what is the instruction manual for activating this Spirit of Christ that is in us? It is the Holy Word of God, the scriptures, and our daily revelations from the Holy Spirit! Meditate on them, for they are our keys to unlocking the mysteries of God that reside in us! We can use every word of God to proclaim and release our soul and body from the world's bondage of darkness, disease, and negativity!

"My son, attend to My words; incline thine ear unto My sayings. Let them not depart from thine eyes, keep them in the midst of thine heart. For they are life unto those that find them, and health to all their flesh." ~*Proverbs 4:20-22, KJV*

One day while conversing with our grandson, the Lord spoke to him prophetically through me: "You have an open book of life laid before you, and you are the one who will write what is on the pages." I also saw a beautiful stream of living water coming toward him. Hallelujah!

"Trust in the Lord with all thine heart; and lean not unto thine own understanding. In all thy ways acknowledge Him and He shall direct thy paths. Be not wise in thine own eyes: fear the Lord, and depart from evil. It shall be health to thy navel, and marrow to thy bones." *~Proverbs. 3:5-8, KJV*

23 WE HAVE A NOW GOD!

During one of the worship services held in our home, the Holy Spirit anointing fell upon us! The Holy Spirit's fire overwhelmed me, and I wanted to share it with others by touching and prophesying over them! As I touched one sister, I saw in a vision, a book of scriptures in her hands. I saw the words coming off the pages as if they were alive. I then prophesied that the scriptures would actually come right off the pages into reality. I did not understand totally what it meant. However, in a few minutes it was revealed. She saw in vision, Jesus coming down to accept and thank us for the songs and praises we were offering up. The Word indeed came off the pages and appeared as Jesus to my sister!

"In the beginning was the Word, and the Word was with God, and the Word was God. The same was in the beginning with God. All things were made by Him and without Him was not anything made that was made. In Him was life; and the life was the light of men." ~*John 1:1-4, KJV*

During this same anointing, I noticed short streams of light descending upon my husband. Also, as I walked toward my grandson, Alex, I spiritually saw water gushing out of his upper belly! At the time I had never heard of such a thing.

That night after the service, the Bible concordance was put into action. Sure enough, there was a scripture confirming what I had observed.

Jesus says: "If anyone is thirsty, let him come to Me and
drink. Who ever believes in me, as the scripture has said, streams of living water will flow from within him" ~*John 7:47-48, NIVB*

The King James Version says "Out of his belly shall flow rivers of living water."

God's truth is very simple yet very deep. We should never approach the knowledge of God through our intellectual and worldly wisdom. Truth can only be understood by the Spirit of God, Who abides in us.

The tense of scripture is present tense because the scriptures are alive! So many times when we look at scripture, we logically look at them in the future tense, or in the past tense, with our minds instead of His "now" Holy Spirit. The Spirit can quicken our understanding. When we read a scripture with the Spirit of God, we are enlightened! If we go back to check it later with our carnal, logical mind, it does not carry the same message. God is omnipresent! His words are alive! Let's look at the seemingly most offered prayer from the Living Word, the Lord's Prayer.

We say, "Thy Kingdom come, Thy will be done on earth as it is in heaven." ~*Matthew 6:10, KJV* I would like to add the word "now." "Thy Kingdom come(now), Thy will be done (now) on earth as it is in heaven."
~*Matthew 6:10, KJV*, inserts mine.

We wait and we wait for a blessing, thinking that we have to suffer all types of terrible conditions because God "wills it!" I have heard many people say, "Oh, I am sick so I will be humbled and love God more!" Or, "I am going through a testing time so I will be stronger!"

Jerry and I did hospital ministry and believe me, God doesn't cause illness, pain, and unhappiness to make people love Him more. This idea of God being responsible for these tragedies is one of Satan's lies. Satan is the destroyer and murder, not God! Go to the hospital and you will see the ravages of the devil's rage against God's people. In my opinion, we give credit to God for things that He doesn't do nor would do.

Now yes, God can bring light and good out of any of our dark experiences. But He never breaks our leg so we will love Him more! You may come to depend upon Him more, which is a good thing. Illness does not bring God Glory. Healing, joy, and peace brings Him Glory.

Illness was the result of the fall of Adam and Eve. It is also part of having corruptible flesh. Let us always remember Jesus is the Resurrection! That resurrection power can raise us into His arms in our darkest hour, and will, if only we believe!

"Thy will be done on earth as it is in heaven." ~*Matthew 6:10, KJV*

Jesus told me that if we want to know what God's will is, all we need to do is look at heaven, for heaven's sake! The Lord's Prayer is asking God for His will to be on earth as it is in heaven, right? So by looking at heaven, we can see what His will actually is.

Are there any sick in heaven? Is there any poverty in heaven? Or is there stress or depression in heaven? Of course not! Now we know what His will is: No stress or depression on the earth, No poverty on the earth, No illness on the earth,

"Thy will be done on earth as it is in heaven." ~*Matthew 6:10, KJV*

No longer pray, "Only if it is Your will," when praying for the ill, the depressed, or the poverty stricken! For we certainly should know what His will is. It is that which is done in Heaven (present tense). Decree instead: Christ's victorious works!

"For our gospel came not unto you in word only but also in power and in the Holy Ghost." ~*1 Thessalonians 1:5, KJV*

All gifts that are present in heaven can be activated here on earth by faith. But we must choose to believe it!

Believe that it is our Eternal Father's desire and plan for His children to have life and have it more abundantly, on earth as it is in heaven!

Sometimes it is not easy to get to the Healer because of our fleshly unbelief. But if we persist we can connect with the faith of Jesus. When I was trying to increase my own faith one time, Jesus told me,"Do not focus on your faith! Focus on My power!"

Focus on Jesus' healing power just like the woman with the issue of blood did. Let's picture her healing: ~Luke 8:4548, NMB, reenactment mine.

There was chaos in the streets! The sounds of people cheering, babies crying, and many men and women shouting out the name "Y'shua" added to the mix! The disciples felt crushed trying to protect their Lord from the sweltering crowds. It was a hot day. They could smell the sweat of others as their own sweat on their faces mixed with the dust from the street. Talk about frustration! And here is Jesus asking them a simple question:

"Who is the one who touched Me?"

Everyone standing close to Jesus denied it. There was a moment of consternation from one of the disciples of Jesus. Peter struggled for calmness as he tried to keep the frustration out of his voice, "Master, the crowds are choking You and pressing in."

Y'shua, (Jesus) said: "Someone touched Me. For I know power has come out from Me."

When the woman saw that she did not escape unnoticed, she came trembling and she fell before Him. She reported before all the people what the reason was that she touched Him, and as she spoke she was healed immediately. Jesus said to her, "Daughter, Your faith has saved you. You must continually go in peace."

Jesus is not willing for anyone receiving the touch of His Spirit to go away empty-handed. He will always be willing to heal you! Our part is to believe, not in our faith, but in the love and healing power of Jesus! We are given the faith of Christ when we are born anew, but we must believe!

It is our fleshly unbelief that keeps us from being healed.

Recently early one Sunday morning, my husband rushed me to the hospital emergency room. I was almost Comatose. He had tried to convince me to go the the emergency room but I was stubborn and wouldn't so he took me anyway.

The doctor could not even get a bottom number on my blood pressure! The top number was 74 and finally the bottom registered 40. (Normal blood pressure is 120/80) I had gotten there just in time. They put me on oxygen. They thought it might be a blood clot in my lung.

But I said out loud to my husband, "No, I do not believe bad reports-only good ones! I choose life, not death." I was confident that a dangerous blood clot was not God's choice! The CAT scan showed there was not a blood clot in my lung, it was double pneumonia instead-a much more manageable illness. Never had I felt so sick. I had not needed a doctor for 15 years, so this was something totally out of my norm. By Tuesday, I was reminding the Lord that He was a mighty God and I knew He wanted to show His glory and mightiness through this event.

"Lord, I know that you are wanting to show me that You are the Mighty God I worship!" I decreed.

He, in-turn, was giving me the knowledge that on Wednesday He was going to perform a miracle! I was listening to Aquila Nash on TV that same Tuesday evening, and she gave a word of knowledge that someone with a terrible infection was going to have God' intervention. I claimed that promise as well, even though I was still feeling extremely sick.

Wednesday Morning I woke up healed! They checked my lungs and they were clear! I felt like a new person! Jerry and I celebrated all of Wednesday by praising the Lord. His Holy Spirit blessed us with a revelation about the reason for my illness. The Lord gave my husband a vision about my ministry! The Lord told us that Satan had tried to destroy me because of my ministry-past and future. He added, "I have a perfect plan for your life and he will not succeed in his!"

The doctors were still were looking for something on Thursday morning. "Maybe you have a damaged liver or liver disease," the doctor announced. I am sure the CAT scan technicians never heard more praising God and speaking in tongues than during that test!

I knew I did not have it! They released me Thursday: A fatty liver but not a diseased one! I had to pay attention to eating fats. That was Jesus' faith, not my own! I wept with joy to be home again! Oh, what a wonder our God is! That was the good side of the story!

After I arrived home, they wanted to be sure that the virus and bacteria had gone. They put me on an antibiotic that gave me a terrible bout of tendonitis, which was noted as a possible side effect of the medicine. I immediately got on telephone and asked for a different antibiotic. But the damage was done!

Now this is the interesting part. I had the faith and belief to be totally healed in the hospital, but at home I could not muster up the belief to get the tendonitis healed! I had dear, spiritual friends come in and pray for me, which not only encouraged me but also relieved a lot of the pain! Six weeks later though I was completely healed! I know that God did not give me tendonitis to love Him more! But I can see that sometimes our belief is weakened by our focus on our pain and the symptoms rather than on Jesus.

Our first response can be panic! It was for me the first time I had tendonitis a year earlier! Fortunately, I recognized panic as the spirit of fear put on me by the devil. So I loudly declared: "Spirit of fear, in the name of Jesus Christ, I cast you out of my thoughts!" It left and never come back.

I was lying at Jesus' feet, spiritually, during that first tendonitis attack, knowing I desperately needed His help, for I was in so much pain! My lack of belief for an instant healing was apparent. I needed a word from the Lord to build up my belief. Remember He always gives a word in the right season, the right time! He is never too late, never too early- just on time!

I said, "Lord just give me a word and I will be healed."

The Lord said to me, "You have a written guarantee."

I answered,"Yes, the scriptures, the promises, your word!"

He resumed speaking, "Signed by My Blood!"

He continued, "I have a warranty deed on you!" In real estate transactions, a general warranty deed is an agreement that the buyer's title to a parcel of land will be defended. A general warranty deed binds the grantor to defend the title against all claims even those arising from previous owners.

Hallelujah! I decreed out-loud all day. I was praising the Lord and saying, "Praise you, Lord, for I have a written guarantee, signed by Your blood, that I walk in divine health. I belong to You, Lord Jesus, even with a warranty deed."

By evening I could get around without that terrible pain. The next day I was well enough for Jerry and I to resume our Thursday prayer ministry at the hospital! Now as you can see I had tendonitis twice. The first time I was healed within two days of my approaching the Lord; the second time took six weeks! What made the difference! The answer lies in my focus! When I expected Jesus to give me a word to increase my belief, I was healed!

"Wherefore be ye not unwise, but understanding what the will of the Lord is!" ~*Ephesians 5:17, KJV*

We must be grounded in knowing His will, His will on earth as it is in heaven. Jesus already paid the price for not only our sins but our healing. But we must know this as the truth. All miracles are available, but we have to believe in Jesus as our answer!

"But let him ask in faith, nothing wavering. For He that wavereth is like a wave of the sea driven with the wind and tossed. For let not that man think he shall receive anything of the Lord." ~*James 1:6-7, KJV*

Remember what the Lord told me: "Do not focus on your faith, but focus on My Power!" Our faith must not be in the belief of the power of *our faith* but in *the faith of Christ* who resides in us! We must believe in the Word which is Jesus!

A while back a conference was held at Springfield, Missouri. I nearly missed my blessing because I was not interested in attending though I felt the Lord entreating me. But a friend wanted to go and needed a ride so I decided to go, solely for her sake. I had been having a type of fog on my brain at times and felt really worn down and old. I never expected anything miraculous to happen there. However, once there, I was very happy I had come, as the ministry of two spiritual giants was amazing. The worship was so wonderful as the melodious sound of the many voices of those who loved Jesus filled the auditorium.

During that worship, a strange looking creature appeared to my right. It was an evil spirit about 12" tall and looked old, putrid gray, and horrible. It also seemed comfortable being there which made me know that it had been with or on me for quite some time. So I spoke and said, "You, get away from me, in the name of Jesus. Go straight to the pit!" Immediately she was gone! I do believe that the power of many believers being unified in their love for Jesus made that experience possible. I praised God that He had made a way for me to be healed, for I felt youthful again.

Recently, My sister's husband passed on to heaven and it caused me such a trauma to see my sister in such emotional pain. It also made my own widowhood more real. I lost my youthful spirit to self pity. Some of my sisters and brothers prayed for me. Several mornings later, I awoke hearing myself *loudly casting off unclean spirits* in the name of Jesus. I had even felt like I had bumped against one of them. I felt a total freedom and my joy returned immediately.

Christ indeed becomes more wonderful than ever as I contemplate: The Living Word, The "Good News," The Cross of Jesus, His Sacrifice, and His Magnificent Love for Us! Glory Hallelujah! He won the Kingdom for us. His Kingdom is in us. He dwells within us and thus, Eternity already is living in us! Glory to God in the highest! Amen!

24 GOD'S WORKSHOP ON HEALING

A number of years ago I was in God's Workshop on Healing and did not even know it, until after it was over. That's when the Lord told me!

We raise black Arabian horses and one of the babies was born with such weak, damaged tendons that it could not get up to nurse on its mother. We had the vet out and he told us there was no way she could overcome this birth defect. He said with that diagnosis, along with the best of hospital care, we were looking at six months for her to heal-and then there was no guarantee she would get better.

At her feeding time, I would go out and hold her up so she could nurse. The rest of the time she was trying to get around on her knees since she could not stand. I cried out to the Lord. Jerry and I were both brokenhearted.

Then I remembered that most of my answered prayers happened after I reasoned with the Lord, explaining to Him why He should do this or that miracle. So I began to tell Him how terrible it would be for this young filly's mother to lose this baby. Literally, I cried brokenheartedly to Him about her. I gave other reasons as well. While I was reasoning with Him, He gave me a very quick vision showing her healed. I was thrilled. I knew the Lord was going to heal her! My husband, on the other hand, did not see the vision. He only saw the baby struggling to crawl around on her knees. I kept saying that I had seen her healed and I knew she would be. Later I realized that though Jerry normally was filled with faith, this time he played the part of the realist. So we went back and forth, not angrily, saying, "I know that God is going to heal her" and "I can't see it."

By Friday of the first week, Jerry was saying, "Vivien, I cannot stand to see that baby struggle like that anymore! If it is not healed by Saturday, I am going to have her put down by the vet!"

Saturday came and the filly started rising herself up on her hooves. By Sunday she was running besides her mother! Jerry and I were absolutely thrilled! The vet was astounded! God had made true His Promise!

I was pondering the whole episode and the Lord told me in His Calm Voice, "You have just been given a workshop on healing."

Jesus lives in us as His Spirit Man!

Jesus loves us!

Jesus sets us up for success. We can "Bask in His Glory."

These are the wonderful truths that I enjoy sharing! I realize more than ever how much Jesus wants to reveal Himself to us-to touch us, to heal us, to satisfy all our longings, and to encourage our troubled hearts. He not only wants us to see His splendor, but He wants us to share it with Him as well! The more experiences we have with Him, the more we love Him, whether He is riding on a cherub or showing Himself as the "Lion of Judah!" This intimate relationship becomes available to us only if we will believe Him to be who He says He is. Believe this, God wants you to visit the heavenly places with Him!

I regretted for years that I was not really free to enjoy the blessings of heaven because of the bondage of precepts taught me by well intentioned teachers.

Everyone was talking about how wonderful it was "going to be" in heaven!

Adam and Eve were created to enjoy heaven in the "here and now"! They lost Paradise and Jesus brought it back. Soon He will come back and cast away the veil of death that covers this earth. Life and Living Water will again spring forth from everywhere on this earth. Until then we will look for the hidden treasures of our Lord.

"And on this mountain the Lord of Host will make a feast of fat things for all people, a feast of wine on the lees, of fat things full of marrow, of wines on well refined lees. And on this mountain He will destroy the face of the covering cast over all peoples, and the veil that is spread over all nations. He will destroy death forever and Adonai, the Lord, will wipe away tears from all faces. And the rebuke of His people will be taken away from the whole earth, for the LORD has spoken it." *~Isaiah 25:6-8, NMB*

God prepares us for success! He arranges divine appointments for the benefit of all those involved in those appointments. A couple of months ago the Lord set us up for a success!

My husband Jerry and I are volunteer chaplains at a local hospital. A few days before our weekly ministry at the hospital, Jerry had horrible pains in his stomach! So I laid my hands on him and began praying. His stomach dropped at least 4 inches under my hands.

I asked, "Jerry, did you feel that?"

He replied, "Yes I did and the pain is totally gone!"

Later that week we went to the hospital to pray for the patients and tell them that God loves them. An Evangelist and his wife were there. He had been planning to go to a foreign mission trip. But here he was in the hospital with a blocked intestine. The hospital had tried many things, yet it remained blocked. He said he was concerned because there was only a short time before it would be too late to leave with his group.

I asked him," Do you mind if I lay my hands on your stomach? The Lord healed my husband's stomach when I prayed for him the other day."

He enthusiastically replied, "No, I don't mind...Please go ahead and pray for me!"

I laid my hands on his stomach, and in the name of Jesus I decreed that the blockage disintegrate into small particles. Jerry added a fervent prayer as well. As we walked through the door, the man was saying, "Call the nurse immediately!"

We went on and prayed for two more people. After we left the second room, the ministers wife was walking quickly toward us! She excitedly declared, "It is a miracle! The minute you went through the door my husband's blockage was completely broken up!"

Jerry and I were thrilled! Now the man knew without a doubt that he was really supposed to go on that mission trip! This miracle caused our belief to grow, not in ourselves, but in Jesus and His willingness to heal! The evangelist, his wife, Jerry, and I all had a wonderful testimony of the faithfulness of our God! I quickly assessed what Jesus had done! He had set us all up for this success!

Since then, He has performed other miraculous healing through our prayers. The more healing happens, the more our belief in Him is enlarged! I wish we had enough belief in Jesus to let it happen much more; however, it is a day to day growth. When we have experiences and share them with others, we are building their belief to have a similar experience!

25 DISCERNING HIS BODY

The Sacrament of the bread and wine (known as Communion or The Lord's Supper) is so sacred to me! I find the most precious words in John. I read these words outloud before I partake of the bread:

"I Am the Bread of Life! Your fathers ate manna in the wilderness and they died. This One is the Bread that descends from heaven, so that whoever would eat of it would not die. I Am the Living Bread that descended from out of heaven; If anyone would eat of this bread he will live forever, and also the bread which I shall give on behalf of the life of the world is My flesh." ~*John 6:48-51, NMB*

"That the Lord Jesus the same night in which He was betrayed took bread: and when He had given thanks, He brake it, and said, 'Take, eat: this is My body, which is broken for you: this do in remembrance of Me.' After the same manner also He took the cup, when He had supped, saying, 'This cup is the new testament in My blood: this do ye, as oft as ye drink it, in remembrance of Me'." ~*1 Corinthians 11 :23-25, KJV*

Then I read from John these precious words of Jesus as I partake of the wine (or grape juice):

"Most certainly I say to you, unless you would eat the flesh of the Son of Man and you would drink His blood, you do not have life in yourselves. The one who chews My flesh and drinks My blood has eternal life, and I shall raise him on the last day. For My flesh is true food and My blood is true drink, The one who chews My flesh and drinks My blood remains in Me and I in him. Just as the living Father sent Me and I live because of the Father, then the one who chews Me, even that one will live because of Me. This is the Bread which has come down from heaven, not just like the fathers ate and died: The one who chews this Bread will live forever." ~*John 6:53-58, NMB*

Hallelujah!

I realize that the Communion of bread and wine is served differently in many different congregations and religions. So my outlook on this sacrament may seem unusual! I prefer taking it with Jerry, by myself, or with a small group. It is a time of pure communion and fellowship with my Lord. My husband spoke in tongues and interpreted it at one Communion service. He was told that partaking of the bread and wine is the "triumphal entry of Christ into our soul!"

I cannot think of a more beautiful description of this Sacrament! We already have Christ in our spirit man. Our taking of the Lord's Supper gives Him entry into our body, mind, and emotions. He renews and refreshes both body and soul! Truly, He continues daily to become greater and more beautiful in our eyes.

Hallelujah!

What a journey we all have through this life! If we open our hearts and listen for the Lord's voice, we will learn by leaps and bounds.

During all those years of attending an organized church, I never heard of the Lord's Supper as a healing sacrament. It is so readily known that the already shed "blood" (the wine) of Christ has paid the price for our sins when we are baptized-past, present and future. His blood has made us righteous and worthy before Him. Never was there a hint, that partaking of His body (the bread) was meant as a reminder that by His stripes and broken body we are healed.

It can be a miraculous healing ordinance of both soul and body! We need to truly meditate on both the bread and the wine and do it with the remembrance of His great sacrifice. As a remembrance so that our souls can be refreshed (blood) and our bodies healed (flesh)! I think it is interesting and must be significant that Christ served the bread first.

Apostle Paul knew that our health was related to taking Communion. He warned the Corinthians about taking the bread and the wine unworthily. Why unworthily? Because they were coming to eat of the bread and drink of the wine lightly, and not "discerning" the body of Jesus that they were partaking of. He told them to eat at home for their physical hunger.

"But let a man examine himself, and so let him eat of that bread and drink of the cup. For he that eateth and drinketh unworthily eateth and drinketh damnation to himself, not discerning the Lord's body. ('This is My Body...' ~1 Corinthians 11:24) For this cause many are weak and sickly among you, and many sleep." *~1Corinthians 11 :28-30, KJV,* insert mine.

A few years before Jerry and I left an organized religion, I discerned the Lord's body at one Communion service in a startling way! The emblems (bread and the wine) were arranged on a table covered with a white cloth. The emblems were handled in a precise way to honor Christ's sacrifice. The pastor was giving the charge about preparing ourselves to take the sacrament and how we were to sanctify ourselves.

While the pastor was delivering this Communion message, I glanced over to the neatly arranged Communion table. However, instead of the emblems, I saw the body of Christ under the white cloth. I thought, "I can't be seeing this!" I looked away and then back again, expecting the vision to be gone. But there He lay as if slain! I wept. Jesus spoke to me lovingly, He said, "Only by My blood are you sanctified!"

The words spoken were as startling and as powerful as

the vision: "Only by My blood are you sanctified!" I never questioned those words, for I knew they were spoken to me by the power of the Almighty God. The vision left when the emblems were uncovered.

The only way we can be sanctified is by His blood which was shed on Calvary's cross! We can put titles before and after our names, we can be the best persons possible, and we can give our lives for others, yet we can never sanctify ourselves. Only by His blood are we made holy and free! Hallelujah!

Our sanctification was completed on the cross and causes us to be holy in God's sight. We do not take Communion to get a new start on a sin-free life, for that is "sin consciousness."

Let me clarify what I mean. Sin-consciousness means we are focusing on our sins. It should be called self-consciousness, in my opinion, because we are totally caught up in our self, our sins, and our performance. If we come to the communion table with our sin-consciousness we are remembering our self not Jesus! He suffered so much for us because of His great love; He should be our focus. True communion with the Lord is like putting our arms around Him and giving Him a hug! It's all about Him.

Our covenant with Jesus is eternal and needs no renewal. "It is finished!" Our part of the covenant is not to be perfect in and of ourselves, but to continue to believe and remain in Jesus! It would be quite presumptuous to expect Jesus to relive the cross in order to renew His part of the covenant He made with us!

If we could only understand that when we are born again and sanctified by Christ's blood, we are seen as perfect before our God! After we finally embrace this truth, we can move on into perfection of our love for God and for one another. Our sanctification, which Jesus paid for, is why He is not ashamed to call us "His brethren."

"For both He that sanctifieth and they who are sanctified are all of one: for this cause He is not ashamed to call them brethren." ~*Hebrews 2: 11, KJV*

He wants to fellowship with us! Surely we can understand this, knowing how precious it is having our family together for fellowship? The shared love of Jesus is what makes us a family! Makes us one! Do we want unity in our churches? We need to rally around Jesus and His precious love, rather than theological concepts!

Communion is for the remembrance of what Christ's love- glory won for us, His children.

"For as much then as the children are partakers of flesh and blood, He also Himself likewise took part of the same; that through death He might destroy him that had the power of death, that is, the devil; and deliver them who through fear of death were all their lifetime subject to bondage." ~*Hebrews 2:14-15, KJV*

All throughout our life, we face our own death, or worse than that, the death of those we love. Until I read the above scripture I did not realize that for many the fear of death is a bondage. Lately, the Lord has been emphasizing (to Jerry) the message which the angels brought to the shepherds. The message which is so phenomenal, but at times overlooked is this: " Man shall not die!" Because of Jesus, we put on a new man that is Eternal! Our spirit man may pass back through the door of flesh but we will leave the body behind only temporarily. And even until we are resurrected, our spirit man and soul are alive in the reality of God!

While we are still in the flesh, we are called to endure in faith, knowing that God is with us. It is not what happens to us that is important but how we overcome through the blood of Christ Jesus. During trying times, we hang on to His robe with both hands and are encouraged by His love for us!

All Christians should be happy people! Jesus not only canceled our sin debt, paid for our healing, gave us everlasting life, but He also made provisions of deliverance from our temptations and addictions. This too must be part of our remembrance on sacrament days.

"For this reason He had to be made like His brothers

in every way, in order that He might become a merciful and faithful high priest in service to God, and that He might make atonement for the sins of the people. Because He Himself suffered when He was tempted, He is able to help those who are being tempted." ~*Heb. 2:17-18, NIVB*

The blood of Christ gives us life! He is life just like the blood in our bodies contains life. His blood and DNA circulates throughout our whole body giving life to every cell. Our heart's throne, where Christ resides, pumps this life through our body. This too was such an exciting truth for me! The body (flesh) cannot exist without the blood. Neither can our spirits exist in eternity without the Infinite Atonement of our God!

Praise God that He has set a pattern for all truths and evidence! He has provided still another way, through taking the sacrament, to be healed both body and soul!

After having pondered on this new concept one evening, the Lord confirmed it when I retired to bed. I could literally feel His blood circulating throughout my body. I told Jerry that it was like my whole body was "buzzing," and it continued doing this for quite a long time. Oh, if we could just believe that God wants us to have a wonderful, beautiful life here on earth, then we would remember and celebrate His great sacrifice of love-often at the Lord's table.

26 FASTING IS REJOICING

Years ago I fasted from food regularly. Some Christians think that fasting can earn them more influence with God. Some believers say it clears their minds and makes them more sensitive to the Holy Spirit. Recently I have come to a deeper understanding of fasting and it motivates me to enter into it again, coupled with prayer.

Some Believers have the false concept that by fasting you can "twist God's arm" until He gives you what you are asking for. I asked God to teach me His ways and His thoughts about prayer and fasting. He showed me some scriptures about prayer and then proceeded to teach me about fasting:

1. Fasting is not to change God's will to fit our circumstance. It is to change our will to His will in every circumstance.

2. Fasting is not to soften God's heart toward us, but to soften our heart toward Him.

3. Fasting is not to make us great in His eyes, but to make Him great in our eyes!

4. Fasting is laying down all our crowns and idols in our life and worshiping *The Great I Am*.

5. Fasting is laying down our carnal, earthy, reasoning mind in exchange for His mind IE the Holy Spirit.

"Let the mind of Christ be in you."~*Philippians 2:5 KJV*

6. Fasting is celebrating our life in Jesus.

7. Fasting is rejoicing in our God, *the Great I Am*!

Isaiah, Chapter 58 is a marvelous read for fasting. God desires that our fasting be all about love. It is a life changer to read God's explanation on fasting. Let us identify the type of fasting that the House of Israel did that displeased God. Verse 5 says:

1. A man afflicts his soul.

2. A man bows down his head as a bulrush.

3. A man spreads sackcloth and ashes under himself.

Jesus said something similar: "Moreover when ye fast, be not, as the hypocrites, of a sad countenance: for they disfigure their faces, that they may appear unto men to fast. Verily I say unto you, they have their reward." ~*Matthew 6:16, KJV*

In *Isaiah 58:7 KJV*, the Heavenly Father asked: "Is this not the fast that I have chosen ? To loose the bands of wickedness, to undo the Heavy Burdens, to let the oppressed go free, and that ye break every yoke?"

Wow, do you see Jesus in the above scriptures? He did all of these. When we deliver the love of God to others through Jesus, they will be set free. Not by us, but by Him Who is in us! This is a way of fasting!

The following list, taken from Isaiah 58:7 shows more of God's ways of fasting

God's ways of fasting:

1.To give bread to the hungry;

2..To bring those who are poor and homeless to your home;

3. To clothe the naked,

4. To help those in your family who are in need. Do not turn your back on them.

I have only shared a part of Isaiah 58, which is a beautiful chapter on fasting. It is a great read.

Through Zechariah the prophet, God asked His people and priests a question about fasting as well. He said: "When ye fasted and mourned in the fifth and seventh month, even those seventy years, did ye at all fast unto me, (for My sake), even to me?" ~*Zechariah 7:5, KJV*, insert theirs.

Then He spoke to them again through Zechariah: "Execute true judgment, and shew mercy and compassion every man to his brother: And oppress not the widow, nor the fatherless, the stranger, nor the poor; and let none of you imagine evil against his brother in your heart." ~*Zechariah 7:9, KJV*

I must confess that this is not what fasting is normally thought to be. This fasting is a way of living! When our hearts are yielded to the pain and needs of others, we are in a state of fasting and grace. When we yearn for all to know the salvation of Jesus, we are in that same state of fasting. It is not about suffering to show ourselves approved. It is yielding our spirit to His Spirit!

Come, rejoice, for we have the Bridegroom with us!

"Then came to Him the disciples of John, saying Why do we and the Pharisees fast oft, but Thy disciples fast not? And Jesus said unto them, 'Can the children of the bride chamber mourn, as long as the bridegroom is with them?'" ~*Matthew 9:14-15, KJV*

We are: "the temple of the living God, as God hath said, *I will dwell in them, and walk in them; and I will be their God, and they shall be My people.*" ~*2 Corinthians 6:16, KJV*

When we are truly fasting and praying, we are not focusing on not eating. Fasting is not a performance if it is sincere. Fasting is natural and automatic for those who are deeply into praying about someone or something. We are so concerned and our heart so broken that we do not care to eat.

Fasting is setting aside a time to give our complete attention to the Heavenly Father: to seek, listen, and receive from Him. Food is the farthest thing from our thoughts. But when we fast as *a performance* or *a sacrifice*, food becomes a constant temptation and battle. It becomes another dead work to pile up for ourselves.

Will our flesh rebel? Yes! But we have the victory over our flesh through Christ Jesus, so we continue.

When I fast, I do not consider what I am doing without but rather Who I have answering my petition: Jesus Christ. I feast on the Bread of Life as a way of fasting from the world's wisdom. I have been baptized by the Holy Spirit and Fire. My Bridegroom King lives in me, therefore I choose to rejoice daily for the love of God. I choose to love others and to live for His purposes in me because He first loved me! Rejoicing in Him is my attitude while fasting!

Fasting is also surrendering to the Lord all that you are or hope to be. Surrendering our all for His All is what it is all about. I had the following experience about that truth.

I had been meditating on surrendering everything in my life to Him and that was my focus for a number of weeks. Yet it was still a surprise one Sunday morning when I was worshiping My King by dancing for Him. We were singing and I was dancing to the song <u>All Hail King Jesus</u>. Then I heard His clear voice, "Stand still." So I immediately followed His command and had an open vision of Him standing before me probably about 5-6 feet away.

The sky is the most beautiful azure blue in my visions. Colors in visions are literally *alive*. Colors here in the natural are caused by the reflection of light but not in the Spirit Realm.

Jesus was standing in a wheat field. The colors of the wheat were rich golds, ochers, and a touch of orange. They contrasted beautifully with the stunning blue of the sky.

But the most magnificent to look upon was Jesus. He was in a simple white gown to just below His knees. His blue eyes were so wonderfully warm, filled with love for me. He caressed the tops of the wheat with His finger tips and smiled sweetly at me. Then He pulled some kernels off the wheat head and opened His hand to show me. He said "A grain of wheat must fall to the ground and die before it is reborn."

I was crying because I was so overwhelmed with joy at His presence, and I answered pleadingly in my Spirit, "Lord, let me be that kernel of Wheat!"

Then I entreated Him. "Please stay a moment longer."

He did stay a moment or two longer, smiled very broadly at me, and then left.

Months later, after that vision, I was meditating on a prayer and fasting scripture Matthew 17:20, because of Dave Roberson's true insight on it.

When the disciples could not cast out a demon on their own and asked Jesus why they could not. His answer:

"Because of *your unbelief,* for assuredly, I say to you, if you have faith as a mustard seed, you will say to *this* mountain. 'Move from here to there,' and it will move; and nothing will be impossible for you. However, this kind (of unbelief) does not go out except by prayer and fasting." ~*Matthew 17:20,21 NIVB,* my italics and parenthesis.

I had meditated on this scripture before but had accepted a traditional teaching that *casting out devils* was the main topic. But then I saw that through Dave's teaching it was *the unbelief* that was the subject of Jesus teaching.

While meditating again on the scripture, the Holy Spirit opened my blind eyes to see for the first time *the mountain* Jesus was referring to *in this case* was *their unbelief.* And so He gave them the key to removing *their mountain of unbelief.*

He told them it was a combination of prayer and fasting, (preferably praying in the Spirit and fasting.)

Now what would fasting accomplish here? Sacrifice is not what the Lord Jesus was speaking about, but placing the flesh under the dominion of our Spirit man. Let's tell the truth, *unbelief* is a Spirit issue that has to be resolved, so the flesh must become dead so our Spirit can be led to a place where we can hear God's voice and invite the Lion of Judah to come in and fight this battle to take away our *unbelief.*

"So then those who are in the flesh cannot please God. But you are not in the flesh but in the Spirit, if indeed the Spirit of God dwells in you...And if Christ is in you , *the body is dead* because of sin, but the Spirit is life because of righteousness (right standing with God)."~*Romans 8: 8-10*

NIV, parenthesis mine.

"Oh, Lord I come before Your throne humbly aware of the privilege of being an adopted daughter and wife of the king, acknowledging *my unbelief,* declaring my body dead to the lusts of the flesh as I enter a season of Praying in the Spirit and Fasting from the flesh including the desire for food. I declare Your name, Your beautiful name for all the universe to hear and declare *that my God does reigns.* I declare the name of *Jesus* to all the firmament."

"Oh, how I love You, and oh, how You love me! That You would sacrifice Your life for me. Such a miracle so profound that I could never comprehend nor speak the magnitude of such sacrifice. That the God of all creation would come down in the form of a man that He might save all His creation. That you might come and answer our plea to come live in us!What a miracle! What words can express or songs speak of that excellency of the living God?"

"Oh Lord, I surrender all to You. I will do what You ask me to do that my joy might be full, and Your joy might be full. Come and fight, raise Your Sword, Your Word and destroy all unbelief and doubt in me, I pray."

We must die to our will and accept His.*"Thy Kingdom come Thy Will be done on earth as it is in heaven."* It is a process that takes time. Be encouraged, the Holy Spirit activates the Spirit of Humility in us.

27 ENTERING INTO HIS GLORY

If you were to ask me what one of my favorite and most beloved things to do, I would have to say, "Worshiping Jesus!" I can turn on a Praise CD's, lift my arms in submission and honor, and enter quickly into *His Throne Room,* spinning around in ecstasy!

Worship is divine intervention between God and man by the Holy Spirit, bringing our Spirit into the divine presence or the Glory-love of God. We can come through the gates with praise and thanksgiving ourselves but Worship can only happen when the Spirit of God reigns supreme. That is why we entreat the Holy Spirit to come. The presence of God is only a step of faith and praise away from us at all times. We ask for God to bring His presence to us, but it is us who needs to take His invitation and step into His presence by inviting the Holy Spirit's intervention by praise and thanksgiving.

Our Lord is available 24/7 for our adoration and praise! I used to mainly thank Him for my blessings,and I still do while praising Him! But when I enter into worship, I glorify Him for who He is, not for what He has done for me! I worship Him because He is so beautiful and lovely. I worship Him for all the love that He is.

My dear friend and sister in Christ Karen Randall had

a new revelation on *praise*. Here are some excerpts from Karen's own written testimony:

"Recently, I had a dream,...I was being taught by the Lord. I was shown that when we worship God through songs of praise and adoration, it blesses Him and it benefits us. **Praising the Lord causes us to REMEMBER who God is. It brings to our memory all of His wonderful, unsurpassed qualities.** We remember that God is Love. He is merciful, kind, forgiving, all-powerful, all knowing, everywhere at all times, in and through all things, gracious, faithful, our Healer... As we are reminded of His matchless love and power, **our faith then is strengthened** so that we can receive even more blessings from His hand...so when we praise Him, His glory (His presence) descends upon us and we are filled with even more rejoicing and praise."

Hallelujah! God manifests His Own Identity through our praise. He is indeed enthroned in our praises, King of Kings, Lord of Lords, Father, Son, and Holy Ghost.

Jerry and I have had marvelous visions of His magnificence while in worship! Worship is not about us! It is all about Him, the Most High God! He wants to reveal Himself to His people! He wants to reveal His love for us! Worship allows our hearts to open up to His revelation!

One time when Jerry and I were worshiping Jesus, as we were listening to the song, "Shout to the Lord," Jerry saw a vision of the Lord. Jesus was wearing His golden crown and walking through the midst of the mountains. As He was walking, the mountains were bowing down to Him and the sea waves were crashing. Jesus was so magnificent! He walked along in complete calmness and peace! Jerry had never seen Him look so glorious as this!

Hallelujah! Jesus does reign!

Going to a traditional church is great fellowship, and if you have a spiritual leader or leaders, you gain new insights.

But for worship it is not always the best vehicle! I look back on what we called "worship" in our church, and it makes me sad how short we came of true worship!

The Spirit of the Living God would come during part of the service, and then it was interrupted by another part of the order of service. In other words, we were only allowed so much time for each part no matter what the Holy Spirit wanted. The hymns were picked ahead of time. Although they were picked often by inspiration of the Lord, there was no member participation in that selection. "Now it is time to do this..." or " Now time for that!" There were Sundays when I felt uplifted and others I felt let down! I can honestly say that worship in those ordered services was nothing compared to the worship we had experienced at home or at our charismatic fellowship!

When we broke away from the traditional church, we started a little worship group in our home. The Lord gave my husband a revelation on worship and we started from there. We absolutely loved the Holy Spirit-led meetings. We met for three and a half years. Our instructions to all those who came were the same: Leave your church doctrines at the door. Leave your cares and worries at the door. This is all about worshiping Jesus! He is the center! (There are some churches where worship is free and there is less of a planned program although there is still wise order.)

The Holy Ghost was in charge of our worship services! We were arranged in a circle so that not one of us was above the other. Every person spoke as they were led by the Holy Spirit. Sister Karen Randall was a guitarist and our worship music leader. She was very sensitive to the Spirit and led us in songs. She had compiled a book of praise and worship songs. Each of us chose the songs we liked. We led out in praise and then the Holy Spirit of worship came. This reminds me of Jesus saying of the Holy Spirit: "He will bring glory to Me by taking from what is Mine and making it known to you." ~*John 16:14, NIVB*

Sometimes in worship services, we get so enthusiastic about our praise that we do not sense when the Holy Spirit wants to enter in and bring worship. Praise is what man is bringing forth. God is always stirred by our praise! However, we need to be sensitive to the Holy Spirit as He leads us from praise into worship. During these times, brassy loudness has no place. The tempo of the music changes and the voices of the singers become softer but more intense in worship, which brings us right into God's Glory!

You know when the Glory arrives, for there is a hush, a breathlessness, as you sense the holiness of God! The heavens open many times, as one of our members literally saw. You wish you could just stay in that Glory forever! Worship and Glory is brought forth by the Most High God, therefore both Worship and Glory are supernatural! God brings forth and facilitates the operation of the heavenly gifts by His Holy Spirit! Many miracles and supernatural blessings occur in the Glory!

Ruth Heflin has written a wonderful book called, "Glory." I read it long after we started our group, and I recognized the steps in it; they were the same as what we, ourselves, had been told to do by the Holy Spirit. Ruth described the same format as ours very clearly. This is an example how the Holy Spirit teaches the same truth to all of us. I highly recommend her book!

True worship like this is wonderful! True worship is Supernatural! The worship at our home was similar to what Apostle Paul described: "How is it then brothers? When you would come together, each one has a Psalm, has a teaching, has a revelation, has a message in a tongue, has in interpretation: all things must continually be toward building up the congregation." ~1 Cor. 14:26, NMB

As a group, and individually, we got so blessed by the Holy Spirit during our meetings in our home! We ate at God's banquet table every Saturday evening-filling up with spiritual food! Namely, JESUS! After we praised, worshiped, and entered the Glory for a time, we would pull out a chair and any member that wanted prophetic prayer or healing would be blessed by other members who felt led by the Lord to lay their hands on them and pray! We called it the *Hot Seat* because of the fire of the Holy Ghost.

"And these signs shall follow them that believe, in My name shall they cast out devils, they shall speak with new tongues...they shall lay hands on the sick, and they shall recover." ~*Mark 16:17-18,KJV*

Jesus invites you to worship wherever you are! You do not need music. Music just works to move some quicker into His presence! Worship is the highest act of honor we can show our Creator God!

If you want revelations, visions, miracles, then worship! If you want to get rid of your stress, then worship! If you want healing of soul or body, then worship! If you want enlightenment for a specific question, then worship!

If you feel a little strange doing this at home, turn to David's psalms to get some ideas for high praise and worship. Remember it is not the glorious words that matter but the love and honor you give the Lord from your heart! Jesus will be thrilled to hear those beautiful words. Find a Praise and Worship CD, if you love music, to help you along. I promise that if you will worship Him in this way, you will be greatly blessed with His Presence. And your spiritual life will grow in leaps and bounds. You will be *Basking in His Glory* shortly!

There are many ways to worship the Lord. David danced before the Lord as worship! I know this is very much shunned by some Christian groups as a form of worship. It depends on your comfort zone. The Israelis and the Messianic Jews still worship today by dancing and singing the words of the scriptures. Dancing is a very meaningful expression of our great joy and love for our Heavenly Father. I enjoy dancing before my King myself.

"Thou hast turned for me my mourning into dancing: Thou hast put off my sackcloth, and girded me with gladness." ~*Psalms. 30:11, KJV*

The following is a word given to me at Antioch Fellowship at Sedalia, Missouri.

The Dancer
by Rick Everitt

    The music drew her from her seat and spoke to her spirit and feet in a language only she seemed to understand.

    The expression on her face was one of pure joy and love for her Lord, and the smile that played across her face seemed to light up the sanctuary.

    Those who played the music and sang the lyrics were moved by her dance and it was reflected in their voices and skill.

    The dancer, absorbed in her worship and her spirit adrift on a sea of love, was unaware of the tears of joy that coursed down the cheeks of all who watcher her.

    Dance is a wonderful expression of worship; with the power to strip away the toils of life, lift the spirit, and bring the dancer to the very foot of the throne.

    Although the anointing heightens the dancer's skill, perfection is not her aim. No, her aim is nothing less than unbridled, unencumbered adoration for the God who gave her life.

This moment in time is what she lives for. Her heartbeat is steady and her spirit fixed on Jesus. The hands on the clock have stopped; the world around her has come to a standstill. There is nothing but the sound of the music and the whisper of angel's wings.

She sees her Lord. A smile is on His face and joy is in His eyes. Their hearts beat as one, she parts her lips to praise, He lifts His hands to bless and all of heaven pauses to bow before the Lamb and to share in His joy.

As the music comes to an end and the stage is cleared, the aroma of sweet incense caresses the dancer's spirit. And what is this? A voice-a beautiful voice, It is His voice and it proclaims, *"Well done, my daughter, well done."*

"And David danced before the LORD with all his might; and David was girded with a linen ephod." *~2 Sam. 6:14, KJV*

"Let them praise His name in the dance: let them sing praises unto Him with the timbrel and harp." *~Psalms 149:3, KJV*

"Praise Him with the timbrel and dance: praise Him with stringed instruments and organs." *~Psalms 150:4, KJV*

"Then shall the virgin rejoice in the dance, both young men and old together: for I will turn their mourning into joy, and will comfort them, and make them rejoice from their sorrow." *~Jeremiah 31:13, KJV*

It is out of our belly (our spirit) that Living Water comes, not our intellect. So it is important when you worship that you drop down into your spirit man rather than your brain. Spiritual is not intellectual; neither is intellectual spiritual! The intellectual is of the flesh! If you lift your hands to worship the Lord, you will automatically drop down into your spirit man. You will worship from your heart.

"Hear the voice of my supplications, when I cry unto Thee, when I lift up my hands toward Thy Holy Oracle."

~*Psalms 28:2, KJV*

"Thus will I bless Thee while I live: I will lift up my hands in Thy name." ~*Psalms 63:4, KJV*

"My hands also will I lift up unto Thy commandments, which I have loved; and I will meditate in Thy statutes." ~*Psalms 9:48, KJV*

"Lift up your hands in the sanctuary, and bless the LORD." ~*Psalms 134:2, KJV*

"Arise, cry out in the night: in the beginning of the watches pour out thine heart like water before the face of the Lord: lift up thy hands toward Him for the life of thy young children, that faint for hunger in the top of every street." ~*Lamentations 2:19, KJV*

"Let us lift up our heart with our hands unto God in the heavens." ~*Lamentations 3:41, KJV*

There are some churches where worship is free and there is less of a planned program. A few years ago before I became widowed, my husband and were worshiping at just such a congregation in Warrensburg, Missouri, when the Lion of Judah showed up again. Oh, how those Children of God loved worshiping Jesus with their voices, keyboards and tambourines all "jiving!"

Hallelujah!

Jerry and I loved being there! Suddenly, I saw the Lion of Judah sitting upright before the podium and pulpit. He was truly enjoying the praise! Then He wandered down the center aisle as happy as could be! The Lord asked me to share this testimony with them, which I did. One man confirmed that he too had seen a lion. He had wondered: "What was a lion doing walking through the empty pews?"

The message the Lord wanted me to convey was this: "I Am very pleased with this congregation because you have praised and worshiped me this morning in such a marvelous way! And because you have done this, I am going to bless this congregation with many blessings."

Jesus fulfilled that promise that very day. A young couple came forward when the alter call was given. We watched joyously as they were baptized into Jesus. It was such a blessing! Each of them had a parent in attendance that day, and each parent had been praying fervently that their child would come forward and be baptized. The baptized couple decided to start their new life in Christ by taking their marriage vows immediately afterward. Hallelujah! Whether He appears as the Lamb or the Lion, our God is a great God! He is such a marvelous Lord and wonderful Savior!

28 THE UNKNOWN LANGUAGE

I want to dwell in the mountain of the Most High God.
I want to dwell in the house of the Most High God.
I want to dwell in the arms of the Most High God.
I want to dwell in the heart of the Most High God!
Hallelujah! He has provided a way: Jesus!
(Tongues with interpretation given to me.)

The first gift God gave the apostles and disciples of Christ at Pentecost was the gift of tongues! Yet, it is in my opinion the most underrated gift of the Holy Spirit! There is much confusion and fear associated with this gift! I would like to deal with some of this fear and confusion. Does the following question sound familiar? "How do I know that I am not cursing God?"

Are you frightened by this question? Be of good courage!

Jesus does not mislead us or deceive us! Things of the Spirit do indeed seem like foolishness to those who are not of the Spirit. It is our earthly life that is the illusion and our spiritual life that is the reality!

Apostle Paul declares to the Corinthians: "The natural man receiveth not the things of the Spirit of God: for they are foolishness unto him: neither can he know them, because they are spiritually discerned." ~*1 Cor. 2:14, KJV*

The Holy Ghost gives us discernment to know that which is good and that which is evil.

Jesus said in the New Testament and He says the same today: "Even so every good tree bringeth forth good fruit; but a corrupt tree bringeth forth evil fruit. A good tree cannot bring forth evil fruit, neither can a corrupt tree bring forth good fruit." ~*Matthew 7:17-18, KJV*

You being *a good tree* would not curse God!

For many years, I heard this: "How do I know that I am not cursing God?" It was not asked as a question but as a condemnation of the gift of tongues. This question infers one of the devil's lies: that we would curse God! Satan hates it when we speak in tongues! He knows that we are speaking a language he cannot translate. He also knows that it is the Holy Spirit speaking on our behalf!

Christ, the Spirit of Truth, has been birthed in us when we are born-again. He helps us discern the truth and keeps us from deception when we seek Him. Whether we speak in our own language or an unknown tongue, He will witness to our Spirit whether it is of Him or not. It is your right and privilege to have this gift of discernment. Whenever you hear something that is supposed to be from the Lord, just ask the Holy Spirit to witness to you if it is from Him or from a lying spirit. He will always show you the truth .Did the visitors from all over the world on the day of Pentecost hear the cursing of God from the disciples tongues? No, the foreigners declared: "We hear them declaring the wonders of God (mysteries of God?) in our own tongues!" ~*Acts 2: 11, NIVB,* insert mine

The disciples were made fun of at Pentecost! They were even accused of drunkenness! Have we ever been in a meeting when the Holy Ghost *slays* people in the Spirit? Have we been tempted to think the same thing?

"It just sounds like a bunch of *gibberish!*"

Have we ever listened to a group of foreigners speaking in another language? I have watched a couple of Jackie Chan's movies on television with my husband. To us Chinese sounded like *gibberish* but they know what they are saying.

Should we be discouraged from speaking and praying in tongues by other Christians? The truth is that the gift of tongues is denigrated by many church organizations. In my opinion, they see the gift of tongues as a weird gift that should never be opened in public and only opened up rarely, if at all, in a closet at home! The pressure of rejection from some Christian groups on their members, if they do anything that is not considered *proper church decorum,* causes many not to embrace this and other precious gifts from the Lord. The lifting up of hands in a church service is *taboo* for many groups as well.

The Lord spoke to Jerry about the gift of tongues one day. The Lord explained that there have been times during church services He has given someone a message to be spoken in tongues. He also gave the interpretation to two or three other people. However, the person with the message was afraid of being criticized...ostracized so he/she kept his/her mouth closed. The message or interpretation was lost. That is how the Holy Spirit is choked out! The Lord explained to Jerry that it was dangerous for those who reject others because they speak in tongues. I truly believe God's message through Jerry. I would add: It is dangerous because they are holding back the blessings of God from His people. Evidently someone needed that message! Jerry agreed that is what God meant by being dangerous. Not that they were going to be punished, but that they were withholding a blessing and harming someone else.

Peter was exhorting those mockers on the day of Pentecost to recognize that this was not a bunch of drunkards speaking: "These men are not drunk, as you suppose. It's only nine in the morning! No, this is what was spoken by the prophet Joel. 'In the last days, God says, I will pour out my Spirit on all people...~*Joel 2:28-29,"Acts 2:15-17, NIVB,* insert mine.

Should it be any different for us? Should not the Spirit of God be poured out upon God's people the same way today? Jesus Himself said, "And these signs will accompany those who believe; In My name they will drive out demons; they will speak in new tongues...they will place their hands on sick people, and they will get well." ~Mark 16:17, NIVB

I believe that if we are in Christ, and He in us, all the gifts of God are available. This is what is on the banquet table, which has already been set before us, when Christ died on the cross and opened the sealed book. Whether we partake of the gifts is up to us! The gifts are not given for our glorification, but for our edification, enjoyment, and to answer our deepest desires. God wants to bless all of us, as these gifts reveal His own nature to us. Symbolically speaking, they are the *cream in the coffee* or the *frosting on the cake.*

"When Paul placed his hands on them, the Holy Spirit came on them and they spoke in tongues and prophesied." ~Acts 19:6, NIVB

"While Peter was still speaking these words, (long after the day of Pentecost), the Holy Spirit came on all who heard the message. The circumcised believers who had come with Peter were astonished that the gift of the Holy Spirit had been poured out even on the Gentiles (who were not yet baptized by water). For they heard them speaking in tongues and praising God." ~Acts 10:44-46, NIVB, inserts mine.

We can spend many laborious hours learning a new language, whether it be French or Spanish. That's why it is exciting that we have this heavenly language given to us freely and supernaturally-a language that the devil cannot translate or repeat!

Jerry's prayer language sounded like a Native American language. Mine, I have no idea. But I recognize that I am repeating some words just like we do in English. My singing in tongues is a different language completely than my speaking one. It sounds very much like a French influenced language.

Many gifts are rejected by religious leaders, because they value only those gifts which edify the whole congregation. The prophetic tongue is given sometimes at a service with a needed interpretation; however, our prayer language is used daily at home to increase and edify our own spirit man. What a disappointment if we could only have the mind of Christ when we were assembled for a meeting and only for the *greater good?* An old concept becoming popular again, in religious and in political realms, is *group salvation!* Salvation is a personal and individual relationship with Christ. It is wonderful when we can come together in groups in worship; there is something special in doing so. However, that does not disallow for individual worship. I cannot emphasize enough the importance of Praying in tongues to expedite your spiritual life.

"But ye, beloved, building up yourselves on your most holy faith , praying in the Holy Ghost. " *~Jude 1:20, KJV*

Paul speaks about both a prophetic message at a Christian gathering and praying at home. "If any man speaks in an unknown tongue, let it be by two, or at the most by three, and that by course; and let one interpret. But if there be no interpreter, let him keep silence in the church; and let him speak to himself, and to God." *~1 Corinthians 14:27,28, KJV*

Paul speaks about our individual prayer language: "For he that speaketh in an unknown tongue speaketh not unto men but unto God: for no man understandeth him, howbeit in the spirit he speaketh mysteries." *~1 Corinthians 14:2 KJV*

"I would like everyone of you to speak in tongues but I would rather have you prophecy, (in the congregation)." ~Corinthians 14:5, NIVB, insert mine.

Is Paul putting down tongues? Definitely not! Paul says this about tongues: "I thank God that I speak in tongues more than all of you." *~1 Corinthians 14:18, NIVB*

"He that speaketh in an unknown tongue edifieth himself..." *~1 Corinthians 14:4 KJV*

Often we are so encouraged by ministers to put upon us the whole armor of God *~Ephesians 6: 11 -17 ,* however, this encouragement rarely, if ever, includes the next two verses which speaks of the praying in tongues.

"Praying always with all prayer and supplication in the Spirit, and watching thereunto with all perseverance and supplication for all saints; and for me, that utterance may be given unto me, that I may open my mouth boldly, to make known the mystery of the gospel..."~*Ephesians 6:18-19 KJV*

Paul is encouraging the Ephesians to pray for all the other saints and for him in tongues so"(the freedom) of utterance may be given me, that I may open my mouth to proclaim boldly the mystery of the gospel."

"But ye, beloved, building up yourselves on your most holy faith, praying in the Holy Ghost." ~*Jude 1:20, KJV*

My husband was the first person I ever heard speaking in tongues! He was given the gift when he was baptized in the Holy Ghost as a young child. He never shared it before our marriage with anyone as he was afraid that even those at the traditional church would think he was insane. Later we renewed our friendship with a couple who spoke in tongues regularly! We enjoyed them sharing in our worship meetings.

Even so, I thought to myself, "Speaking in tongues is alright for them, but not for me!"

However, after reading on the internet about the advantages of speaking in tongues, and after corresponding with Dr. Paul Richardson, I changed my opinion and began to desire that gift! I prayed and asked God about receiving it. A few weeks later an Irish song came to my mind, "Danny Boy." I had always loved that song. I opened my mouth and instead of English, I sang in another beautiful language. Oh, how I loved to sing that song in my new language. Ever since then, I have been praying and singing in tongues.

When I pray in private to ask God to bless someone, I pray first in English and then I allow the Holy Spirit to intercede for that person through my prayer tongue. The Holy Spirit knows all things and guides us in all things.

Therefore, He knows exactly what the condition is of the person I am praying for and knows much more than I what is needed. What a Blessing! Again, Jesus is doing the work in us and on behalf of others. If I am giving a prophetic blessing by the laying on of my hands, I always ask the person getting the blessing permission to pray in tonguesbefore doing so.

"Likewise the Spirit also helpeth our infirmities: for we know not what we should pray for as we ought: but the Spirit itself maketh intercession for us with groanings which cannot be uttered. And He that searcheth the hearts knoweth what is the mind of the Spirit, because He maketh intercession for the saints according to the will of God." ~*Romans 8:26-27, KJV*

The tongue is one of the most powerful tools we have from the Lord. He spoke into being a literal earth for us! He used His tongue to speak to the prophets so they could write His love letters, the scriptures to us! When I explain tongues to others, I always explain that we lay our self down to Him but sometimes we forget to surrender our tongue to Him as well.

Isaiah surrendered his lips (referring to speaking, so in a sense,he surrendered his tongue). Look what happened to him. He had a grand vision! He was in the throne room of God! Being overwhelmed by this beauty and holiness of God, He said: "Woe is me! for I am undone; because I am a man of unclean lips, and I dwell in the midst of a people of unclean lips: for mine eyes have seen the King, the Lord of hosts." ~*Isaiah 6:5, KJV*

Isaiah did not say "Woe is me, my body is unclean." He said his lips were unclean! He knew that what came out of them was unclean because what he spoke was an indicator of what was in his heart. So what happened?

"Then flew one of the seraphims unto me, having a live coal in his hand, which he had taken with the tongs from off the altar: and he laid it upon my mouth, and said, 'Lo, this hath touched thy lips; and thine iniquity is taken away, and thy sin purged.'" ~*Isaiah 6:6-7, KJV*

Then God asked, "Whom shall I send, and who will go for us?" Isaiah answered, "Then said I, here am I; send me." *~Isaiah 6:8, KJV*

If we surrender our tongue to the Lord for Him to use, we can be a mighty instrument in His hand! Your sins are purged by the baptism of the Holy Spirit, and the evidence is that your tongue now belongs to the Holy Ghost. Trusting God with your tongue shows mighty faith!

Remember what I said about never a dull or boring moment with the Lord Jesus? Well that is true. Many people picture our Heavenly Father as solemn, stern, dull, arrogant, angry, and judgmental. Nothing could be farther from the truth! Our Beloved God is full of life, light, joy, creativity, and unconditional Love. He also has a sense of humor as I have found a number of times. At least He has made me laugh, as I will explain to you next!

"Then our mouth filled with laughter, and our tongue with singing.." *~Psalms. 126:2, KJV*

Jesus said, "Blessed are ye that weep now, for you shall laugh." *~Luke 6:21 KJV*

On one particularly beautiful spring day, Jerry and I were going to pick up horse feed at a grain elevator 22 miles away. We loved driving through the country. We had switched our car with our son's work truck for the day. Jerry is a great driver, so we always enjoy gazing around during this drive. However, Jerry had been having trouble with his eyes (due to a cataract) and the truck steers differently than our car, so ironically as you will soon see, I asked him to please be careful and watch the road closely. This was unusual as I am so comfortable with his driving.

For a little background: You know how sometimes we pray for something and then forget that we prayed for it until it happens? Well, the day before our little excursion, I had gone to the Lord and said, "Lord, I have been singing, praising you, and praying in tongues for a long time now. I have no doubt about it myself, but I wish you would give me an indisputable testimony of tongues so I can share it with others."

We had our windows open as we traveled to the Farmer's Elevator. The scent of the pastures was enjoyable. We began as usual with discussing how awesome the Lord is; then we started praising Him with tongues. We were about 10 miles from our destination when Jerry stopped speaking in tongues and listened to my praising in tongues. I decided I would be quiet too. I turned to say something to him in English, but no English would come out, only tongues. This was such a shock that I waved my arms at Jerry and pointed to my mouth, hoping he would turn his head and see what was happening to me! I tried to say, "Jerry!" But I could only speak in my Spirit language. Jerry, in the meantime, was paying attention to the road because of his eyesight, and he just assumed I was waving my hands because I was really enjoying praising in tongues.

Suddenly, I came to the realization that I could not go into the feed store, order grain, and pay for it because I could not speak English! The farm elevator clerks were not going to be able to translate a language that even I could not translate. Jerry was used to me doing the book work while he helped load the grain. So I tried again to get Jerry's attention by hitting our checkbook on the seat. He would have to go in and order this time, but he only heard the sound of tongues, so he never paid any attention to me.

By this time the whole situation became absolutely hilarious to me. I started laughing while still speaking in tongues. About 5 minutes from our destination, I got my English tongue back! I told Jerry what had happened to me. We both laughed all the way home because of it. And I have to admit, I still laugh about it! I will never forget it nor forget the testimony!

The Holy Ghost is such a fabulous teacher. He makes learning fun! And now I have had the privilege of sharing my indisputable testimony with you! I hope you enjoyed that story as much as I enjoyed living it!

Hallelujah! We have an awesome Lord!

I was amazed when I did an internet search on the gift of speaking in tongues. There are so many fathers and mothers of the faith that were propelled into their miraculous ministry by praying in tongues. John G. Lake is just one of many that mentions that praying and speaking in tongues was the turning point in his ministry. There are too many to even mention here.

Praying in tongues an hour or more a day will propel you to walk in greater Power in the Holy Spirit. Praying in tongues has been shown to actually improve your immune system.

I pray in tongues while I am doing my house work and especially while driving anywhere. I can even pray in tongues when I am studying the word as it is not me doing the speaking but the Holy Spirit through me.

If I am afraid or stressed I pray in tongues and immediately I am relaxed.

When I am praying for others, I will ask them if they mind me praying in tongues because as soon as I begin praying in God's Love Language, the presence of the Lord enters into my soul and I am given the interpretation of what I am praying over them. If you want to experience the power of the Spirit of God, pray in tongues!

If you desire the gift and cannot seem to speak in tongues after much effort and prayer, perhaps you need to ask Father to baptize you in the Holy Spirit to be sure you have been baptized by Fire. Remember the disciples could heal the sick and cast out demons yet had not yet been baptized by fire until Pentecost. It does not hurt to ask and be sure of that Baptism of Fire.

29 ANGELS, ANGELS

Her pure yellow hair was shocking! It reminded me of some people who color their hair in fluorescent colors. My mind was reeling with the reality of an angel with that color of hair. I saw her on one of the Thursdays my husband and I ministered as chaplains at a near by hospital. I was laying my hands on a patient's head and giving her a blessing when the angel appeared. Her robe was a simple white one with a braided gold belt. The same time I saw the angel, the Lord spoke to me, "Tell her, (indicating the lady I was giving a blessing to) you see the angel, and that I have told you to tell her that the angels name is Grace."

I told the patient: "I just saw an angel beside you."

The patient asked, "Oh, the one with the bright yellow hair?"

I answered, "Yes!"

"Oh," She elaborated, "She was with me when I was in the S. Hospital."

"The Lord just told me to tell you that I saw her and that her name is Grace," I continued.

"Oh," she repeated happily, "Her name is Grace! I wondered what her name was."

Now, 6 years later, I heard a wife of a well known Prophetic Evangelist describe the angel in detail and her name was Grace too.

Angels come in a great variety of appearances and sizes. In fact many of them do not have wings which troubled me at first. But I found out later that this was normal. Only certain types have wings. I have read several experiences of other Christians who have seen angels taller than buildings. One day my husband was resting in the sanctuary part of our church home; he saw about ten angels the size of birds. They were flying around for a few moments and then they disappeared.

Because of the Fathers great love for us; He sends us angels to minister to and watch over us. From Genesis to Revelation, angels have had an important part in the lives of mankind.

Abraham a man of great faith sent his servant to find a wife for his beloved son Isaac. Abraham assured his servant with confidence, "He shall send His angel before thee, and thou shalt take a wife unto my son from thence." ~*Genesis 24:7, KJV*

Angels appear and reappear throughout Bible history. Daniel was saved because an angel closed the mouths of the lions when Daniel was imprisoned in a lion's den. *Daniel 6:22, KJV*

"And the Lord sent an angel, which cut off all the mighty men of valour, and the leaders and captains in the camp of the camp of the King of Assyria." ~*2 Chronicles 32:21, KJV*

The angel Gabriel introduces himself to Zacharias:"I am Gabriel, that stand in the presence of God; and am sent to speak unto thee, and to shew thee these glad tidings." ~*Luke 1:19, KJV*

Gabriel was also sent from God to the virgin Mary, presenting God's plans for her. He announced that she was going to become the mother of the Son of God.~*Luke 1:26-35, KJV*

I am sure most of us have heard of many present day experiences where people have seen or heard the voices of angels. Many of us have heard angels joining in the singing of praise songs during worship.

Our hospital ministry I was often accompanied by angels appearing. Again each different from another. I remember being surprised while giving a blessing seeing the chest and abdomen of a warrior angel. He was wearing armor. One time I saw the main hospital doctor being followed by an entourage of angels. They appeared in exquisite white apparel. Wow!

Angels are so important in our lives. We are often astounded when we see or hear them. However, no matter how great the mighty feats they do for us and others, we do not worship them. We thank our Heavenly Father for creating such beautiful and exquisite beings!

Hallelujah!

30 THE SEVEN EYES OF THE LORD

"For behold the stone that I have laid before Joshua; upon one stone shall be seven eyes; behold, I will engrave the graving thereof, saith the Lord of hosts, and I will remove the iniquity of that land in one day." ~*Zechariah 3:9, KJV*

What a fascinating scripture! Its mystery has intrigued me for years. Yet now as the revelation of God is coming forth upon the earth, more is revealed to me. As I began writing this chapter, the Lord began uncovering the hidden manna in *Zechariah 3:9* so I might share it with you!

[Note: Please be patient as I am going to have to quote and paraphrase many scriptures!]

"I will engrave the graving thereof, saith the Lord of hosts." ~ Zechariah 3:9, KJV

The Lord Himself engraved seven eyes on the stone laid before Joshua the high priest. Can we all agree that the only other stones that were engraved upon by God were the Ten Commandments, the Law of Moses? ~*Deuteronomy .9:10* This stone laid before Joshua the high priest is a picture of Jesus! There are so many aspects of this seven-fold Holy Spirit described here that it is difficult to put them in sequence!

Let's look at *Zechariah 4:9-10*. Here Zerubbabel has a plummet in his hand. A plummet is what carpenters use to make sure that everything is perfectly straight and in line. It is a string with a weight or a stone tied to the end of it. If you want to hang wall paper or place a board straight vertically, you use a plummet, or a *level*. Some of us have sung the song about "the man that built a crooked house." He was a man who did not use a plummet! Curiously, we see something on the stone at the end of Zerubbabel's string!

"... Those seven; they are the eyes of the Lord, which run to and fro through the whole earth." *~Zechariah. 4:10, KJV.*

Zechariah 3:9 says: "...the stone that I have laid before Joshua; upon one stone shall be seven eyes..."

Zerubbabel's plummet had the same stone as was set before Joshua. Jesus is the plummet stone. He is the Perfect One that everything else can be measured by. As an Artist I often use a tool called *a square*. If things are not *square* the bottle or window an artist is painting will be crooked.

"...Jesus Christ, Himself being the chief corner stone; In whom all the building fitly framed together groweth unto an holy temple in the Lord; in Whom ye also are builded together for an habitation of God through the Spirit." *~Ephesians 2:20-22, KJV*

This stone, Jesus, was to change history! "...And I will remove the iniquity of that land in one day." *~Zechariah 3:9, KJV*

Christ was crucified and possibly ascended into Paradise to open the sealed book in one day! Look closely at the slain Lamb: "...And in the midst of the elders, stood a Lamb as it had been slain having seven horns and seven eyes, which are the seven Spirits of God sent forth into all the earth." *~Revelations 5:6, KJV*

Now the stones with the engraved Ten Commandments have been replaced by the engraved Corner Stone, Jesus. The law is obsolete and fulfilled by Christ. Zerubbabel brought forth the chief corner stone for the temple; so also the heavenly Father brought forth the Chief Corner Stone, Jesus, "...crying,'Grace, grace unto it.'" ~*Zechariah. 4:7, KJV*

This Corner Stone, Jesus, is for us who are His Temple! The Gospel of "grace, grace unto it..." is fully evident today! Jesus has put all kingdoms under His feet: "Thou sawest till that a Stone was cut out without hands, which smote the image upon his feet that were of Iron and Clay, and brake them (kingdoms of the earth) to pieces." ~*Daniel 2:34, KJV*,insert mine.

The devil tempted Jesus to commit suicide and mocked Him. He said, "Cast thyself down from hence." ~*Luke 4:9, KJV* He was reminding Jesus of the Old Testament Law of "casting stones." The devil wanted mankind to remain under the curse—the law of the Old Testament.However, Jesus, being the Chief Corner Stone of the New Covenant, resisted the temptation.

"Wherefore: Because they sought it not by faith, but as it were by the works of the law. (The Law of Moses) For they stumbled at that stumbling stone (Jesus); As it is written, Behold, I lay in Sion a stumbling stone and rock of offence: and whosoever believeth on Him shall not be ashamed." ~*Romans 9:32-33, KJV*, insert mine!

Joshua the high priest, on the other hand, is a picture of us standing in God's grace: "Now Joshua was clothed with filthy garments , (us before baptism) and stood before the angel. And he (the angel of the Lord) answered and spake unto those that stood before him (heavenly beings?), saying, 'Take away the filthy garments from him.' And unto him he said, 'Behold, I have caused thine iniquity to pass from thee, and I will clothe thee with change of raiment.' (This is what happens to us after we are born again by the Holy Spirit and Fire.) And I said, 'Let them set a fair mitre (a crown-*Revelations 3: 11)* upon his head.' So they set a fair mitre upon his head, and clothed him with garments. And the angel of the Lord stood by. And the angel of the Lord protested unto Joshua, saying, Thus saith the Lord of hosts; If thou wilt walk in My ways, and if thou wilt keep My charge, then thou shalt also judge My house, and shalt also keep My courts and I will give thee places to walk among these that stand by (Heavenly beings?).'" ~*Zechariah 3:3-7, KJV,* inserts mine.

[Note: I realize that it is purely supposition, but could Joshua have been standing among the sons of God who congregated at times before the throne, "among these that stand by?" And if so, was the Lord prophesying of man's prior position in the kingdom to be returned after the day that iniquity was taken away by Christ?]

The above verses in Zechariah Chapter 3 is reminiscent of theseven promises given to those who overcome, recorded in Revelations Chapters 2 and 3. The promises are given to those who confess Jesus as their Lord. Those who dwell in the Grace of God by the Blood of the Lamb and endure to the end are blessed with these promises:

1. We can eat of the tree of life in the midst of the Paradise of God.~ *Revelations 2:7*

2. The second death will have no effect on us. ~*Revelations 2: 11*

3. To those who overcome, "I will give to eat of the hidden manna, and will give him a white stone, and in the stone a new name written, which no man knoweth saving he that receiveth it." ~*Revelations 2:17*

4. "To him I will give power over the nations...And I will give him the morning star." ~*Revelations 2:26, 28*

5. "The same shall be clothed in white raiment; and I will not blot out his name out of the book of life, but I will confess his name before My Father, and before His angels." ~*Revelations 3:5*

6. "Him that overcometh will I make a pillar in the temple of My God, and he shall go no more out: and I will write

upon him the name of My God, and the name of the city of My God, which is New Jerusalem, which cometh down out of heaven from My God; and I write upon him My new name." ~*Revelations 3:12 KJV*

7."... I grant to sit with Me in My throne, even as I also overcame, and am set down with My Father in His throne." ~Revelations 3:12

It is the Spirit of the Living God that will accomplish all these things:"Not by (man's) might, nor by (man's) power, but by My Spirit, saith the Lord of hosts." ~*Zechariah 4:6, KJV*, inserts mine.

But what are these seven eyes of God that are symbolically engraved on the stone? They are spoken of in a number of places besides the above scriptures already mentioned.

"For the eyes of the Lord run to and fro throughout the whole earth, to shew Himself strong in the behalf of them whose heart is perfect toward Him." *2 Chronicles 16:9, KJV*

"A land which the Lord thy God careth for: the eyes of the Lord thy God are always upon it, from the beginning of the year even unto the end of the year." ~*Deuteronomy11 :12, KJV*

"...Grace be unto you, and peace, from Him which is, and which was, and which is to come; and from the seven Spirits which are before His throne. " ~*Revelations 1:4, KJV*

"...These things saith He that hath the seven Spirits of God." ~*Revelations 3:1, KJV*

"And out of the throne proceeded lightnings and thunderings and voices: and there were seven lamps of fire burning before the throne, which are the seven Spirits of God." ~*Revelations 4:5, KJV*

My husband had a vision of the Bride of Christ: "I see the Bride of Christ again. I see her veil hanging down to her shoulders. The top of the veil is crusted with large pearls. She wears a shawl (a cloak) with seven eyes. These seven eyes are the seven Spirits of the Holy One." ~From my husband's transcribed vision, "I Will Cherish Her Forever."

"... A Lamb as it had been slain, having seven horns and seven eyes, which are the seven Spirits of God sent forth into all the earth." (Rev. 5:6, KJV,

For a long time I pondered on the seven Spirits of God mentioned in these scriptures. I had learned from others that most experts considered them to be the Spirits listed in Isaiah: the Spirit of the Lord, the Spirit of Wisdom, the Spirit of understanding, the Spirit of counsel, the Spirit of might, the Spirit of knowledge, and the Spirit of the fear of the Lord. ~Isaiah 11 :2

I went to bed 9:30 p.m. one Sunday evening. Before I went to sleep, I asked God to give me the true meaning of the Seven Eyes and Spirits of the Lord. I did not want to use my carnal reasoning. Immediately after I went to sleep, I had a dream. I was cutting a piece of meat into equal pieces. I woke up minutes later during this process of cutting the meat. Lying there awake I thought disgustedly, "What in the world is this about?"

Then the Lord began to speak to me.

I thought,"Oh, okay, this has a spiritual meaning. Meat means spiritual food."

The Lord calmly asked me "Does each slice have the same makeup as the whole?"

And I said, "Yes, Lord, it is the same!"

He continued,"Do you see that all the slices together are still the whole?"

And I answered, "Yes, Lord, I see that."

He went on to teach me: "So it is with the Seven Eyes of My Spirit!"

The scriptures are true and so simple! The Seven Eyes (Spirits) of God are one and the same! They are the same together or apart! The Lord explained to me that the word "same" in this context does not mean "identical." You can have identical twins, yet they are not the "same." I tried to find another example of "sameness" like the Seven Eyes of God, but I found not one such thing, because this "sameness" is supernatural. The Father, Son and the Holy

Spirit are one of the "same"together and they are One while separated at times. God's ways are marvelous and far above ours! Man may try to explain them into "Three having one purpose," or "One in three separate persons," but the truth of it is;

God is beyond our finding out!

I praised the Lord for a long time that evening, for He truly cares about every little thing about us. That is the purpose of the Seven Spirits of God. They are here to care for His creation!

I told the Lord that I believed in Him so much. I was not surprised to receive an answer from Him, but I was still thrilled that He took time to satisfy my eagerness to know. I declared I was so blessed beyond words just to know Him! He is so wonderful and so awesome; His ways and thoughts are so far above ours. He is higher than any one's thoughts could conceive! And I love Him more than anything in my life

After I finished praising Him, I felt Him slip a ring on the ring finger of my right hand. It was a light colored stone and difficult to describe, since it happened so quickly. I tried to comprehend why He did this, but could not. I felt it there for about an hour but could not see it. This experience still remains a mystery to me. One day while Jerry and I were ministering at the hospital, I felt the ring again, distinctly. I was led by the Holy Spirit to ask for special favor for all the patients that day. All I can do is repeat what Paul said: "O the depth of the riches both of wisdom and knowledge of God! How unsearchable are his judgments, and His ways past finding out! For who hath known the mind of the Lord? or who hath been His Counselor?" ~*Romans 11:33-34, KJV*

Other scriptures to consider:

"Doth not He see my ways and count all my steps?" ~*Job 31:4, KJV*

"For His eyes are upon the ways of man, And He seeth all his goings." ~Job 34:21, KJV

"For the ways of man are before the eyes of the Lord, And He pondereth all his goings." ~*Proverbs 5:21, KJV*

His Wisdom and His gifts are available to all of us who love Him. Just ask. He loves us with an unconditional eternal love.

"Come!" The Bridegroom invites us: "Come and partake of that which I have prepared for you!"

31 THE COMING OF THE SONS OF GOD

Tears flooded my eyes as I listened to Michael W. Smith's CD. The anointing of the Holy Ghost fell on me.
    A vision followed:
    I saw a huge number of people like a cloud hovering above the earth. There were so many of every age, gender, and race. Bright colors of light flashed in and around them. The Lord indicated to me that these individuals had chosen to live at this particular moment in time! They had chosen to come down to earth to be God's instruments, specifically to show forth His Glory, His Love! The Holy Spirit indicated these persons shown to me in the cloud are in reality living on the earth now! They are willing to submit and lay down all of themselves so that He can be their King-their everything.
    I emphasize that Jesus being glorified is their greatest desire. They are laying down every crown they have: fame, fortune, priestly authority, glamor, honor, recognition, and more. They are giving all to be God's instruments. They have been taught through the years by the Holy Spirit how to lay these things down. Now at this time God has re-awakened them to the path they have chosen.
    When the scales were peeled from my eyes in a

moment, I saw the magnificence and the magnitude of this movement! What can I say?

I told Jerry, "This is bigger than you and I; this is bigger than any small group of people; this is the biggest movement of God that we could ever imagine. I say, 'Glory Be To The Lamb!'"

The importance of understanding God's plan for us is vital! We must find out who we are in Christ Jesus before we can continue the perfect plan God has for each of us! God had given a single man, John the Baptist, the prophetic gift of Elijah. John, filled with the spirit of Elijah, prepared the way for the Lord's first coming.

During this dispensation, just before His final return, Jesus is releasing the fullness of Himself into new wine skins: those who have emptied "self" out so they can become new- filled with Him. The Lord gave me the following message a couple years ago:

"I am doing a new thing! I do not put new wine in old bottles! Pouring out the old wine is not enough. You must become a new creature in Me. For only new bottles can hold the new life that I am going to fill you with: My Life! You will be filled with Me-with My love! You will speak My words. You will think My thoughts! I Am the wine of God; I Am the new wine that the old wineskin cannot receive." (I found out later this last sentence had been given in Mitt Jeffords' writings.)

Your age, gender, or race has nothing to do with your being a new wine skin. It is your willingness to allow God's love and righteousness to transform your life. The sons of God, or the bride of Christ or the general term "man" in the Bible does not suggest gender. Apostle Paul wrote: "There is neither Jew nor Greek, there is neither bond nor free, there is neither male nor female: for ye are all one in Christ Jesus. And if ye be Christ's, then are ye Abraham's seed, and heirs according to the promise." ~*Romans 3:28-29, KJV*

We are called to be the "sons of God."

"For as many as are led by the Spirit of God, they are

the sons of God." ~*Romans 8:14, KJV*

These instruments of God's love shall prepare the way for Christ's victorious coming. It is through them that Jesus will reveal His Glory-Love. We are all invited to be His bride if we are willing. He has called us out for such a day as this.

"Creation waits in eager expectation for the sons of God to be revealed!" ~*Romans 8:19, NIVB*

When we lay our self and our self effort at the foot of the cross, embrace Christ's righteousness, and worship Him, we are in the Grace Zone. God's work in us and on us begins immediately. We move from the understanding of His finished work and resurrection to knowing that we have His power in us.

"And if the Spirit of Him who raised Jesus from the dead is living in you, He who raised Christ from the dead will also give life to your mortal bodies through His Spirit, who lives in you." ~*Romans 8: 11,NIVB*

Once we begin to understand the magnitude of Christ's opening of the sealed book, the Life of God in us and our understanding of the meaning of our individual lives quickly matures and deepens. The "fullness of God," which was released with the sealed book, remains available to all who believe in Jesus as their Savior! This "fullness of God in us" gives us a glimpse of what Adam and Eve gave up in exchange for this dark planet.

We are "the temple of the living God, as God hath said, *I will dwell in them, and walk in them; and I will be their God, and they shall be My people.*" ~*2 Cor. 6:16, KJV,* capitalization theirs)

I wish to clearly declare at this point: There is only one true God! No one can ever become Him! We can be filled with His fullness through the baptism of the Holy Spirit but never become Him. There is the Only Begotten Son who is Emmanuel. We can never become the Only Begotten Son either! However, we can be just like Him, which is our Heavenly Father's plan for us. There is only one so if anyone declares anything other than this, we must walk away!

"For I Am God, and there is none else; I Am God, and there is none like Me!" ~*Isaiah 46:9 KJV*

This chapter is **not** about the exaltation of man or flesh! This **is** an exaltation of our great God, King of kings, and Lord of lords! This is all about His love! This is about being instruments of love who bring the gospel of grace to their brethren and exalt the Love-Glory of the Father.

Oh, how our God wishes to uplift the hearts of His beloved people. He wants the discouraged, the sick, the hurting, the discomforted, the despairing, and the lost to be lifted up by His love-power! This is the reason for this movement!

"Behold, what manner of love the Father hath bestowed upon us, that we should be called the sons of God; therefore the world knoweth us not, because they knew Him not." ~*John 3:1, KJV*

The spirits of darkness are everywhere on this planet. They bring misery, death, and despair to all. They have been already defeated by Jesus, but the sons of God need to manifest their defeat as well! Jesus bought our original inheritance back for us. However, we have not moved in to take possession!

"...For this purpose the Son of God was manifested, that He might destroy the works of the devil." ~*1 John 3:8, KJV*

Love, Light, and Glory are synonymous! Darkness is an entity that cannot survive when the glorious light of God is turned on!

"Thou wilt shew me the path of life: in Thy presence is fulness of joy ; at Thy right hand there are pleasures for evermore." ~*Psalms 16: 11, KJV*

Hallelujah!

This calling to be a son is not about Lordship, ruling, or becoming gods! This is about being the manifestation of God's Pure, Holy, and undefiled Love. Only by His love can we and the world be transformed and conformed into His image!

Neither do the sons of God become angels. Angels are a specific creation of the Lord. Lucifer (Satan) was an angel. Satan never was a brother to Jesus. Satan is a *fallen angel*. I point these truths out so my viewpoint will remain clear. What I am presenting as the sons of God is not to be confused with some church's false doctrines.

One day as I was writing at the computer, the Lord began to speak to me about His real purpose for creating us. He explained how from the very beginning we were being prepared for son-ship!

The Second Adam, Jesus, came to pay for the sins of the first Adam! We were created in God's own image! Jesus was the *prototype* of the *new Adam,* the *new man*! We will never learn what we gained by the event that took place in Revelation 5 until we understand what we first lost!

He the Lord fashioned us to become His adopted children whom He can love and cherish. He wants a family. He wants to share all His creative gifts and knowledge with us. He wants to be a Father and plan with us, our future upon and beyond this earth. He told me how He had created a perfect plan for each one of us. He has created us to become just like Him, just like the Only Begotten Son. Yet, He created each one of us uniquely in our own way. We would be unique, but each one of us would be filled with God's love and have the same *form type* as Jesus.

In relating this to Jerry, I said,"I wonder if Mitt Jeffords ever received this enlightenment. For 'what' I am receiving from the Holy Spirit is beyond my expectation. It is phenomenal!"

I needed confirmation from another source. I went back to Mitt's file. I was thrilled. Mitt had a whole chapter on this subject. Shortly thereafter, I was flipping through Revelation on another topic when I happened to see some startling scriptures confirming this concept.

"To him that overcometh will I grant to sit with me in My throne, even as I also overcame, and am set down with My Father in His throne." ~*Revelations 3:21 KJV*

Those who choose to become filled with the fullness of

God, God's love, are being prepared and have been prepared to participate in the greatest revival of all times! The miraculous that we see today is more than it has been seen before. However, this is only a sampling of the power of Christ that is going to be manifested through the sons of God upon the earth!

In the meantime, let us recognize the calling of God on our life is to be His Ambassador. This reminds me of a vision of dead trees that I had.

I had been having quite a few visions and some of them which flashed by, I had dismissed because they might not be of God. But then I decided I might be missing out on the ones He sent to me, so I decided to look more carefully at each of them.

A vision floated into my spiritual vision one morning. It was repulsive so I was expecting something not of God. What I saw were oval shapes which had been split and a putrid deep purplish brown colored liquid was flowing out of them. I looked further, and I weep now recalling what I saw. It was the feet of Jesus crushing the grapes. The words of Isaiah 63 came to my mind. "I have trodden the wine press alone." The foot of Jesus was also crushing the serpent's head! Read Genesis 3:15, Isaiah 53:12.

Then I saw a huge tree! It appeared to be dead and I said to the Lord, "I see a dead tree. It is very large with lots of branches that also dead. What is the meaning of it?"

"The fountain of living water is flowing out of you. Water this tree! Look!"

Then I saw an immense line of dead trees.

"You are my water bearer," He said. "The trees cannot bear fruit when they are dead. You need to water them and bring them life, My Life!" He then smiled at me and commanded, " Look now!"

I looked, and was shocked with what I saw. The dead trees had been transformed into an orchard. They were covered with lush green leaves and had beautiful yellow,red, and purple fruit.

"Now," the Lord spoke so sweetly," do you still believe

your ministry is ineffective? These trees are yours, given to you by Me. Go forth and water them!"

I rejoiced and said, " Hallelujah, Dear Jesus, Thank You!"

Jesus tread the wine press alone. He slayed the Dragon alone. All the work is done. All we need to do is to bring the *Living Water,* Jesus, to the trees!

One morning I woke up in an open vision. I was aware as soon as I awoke that Jesus the King of Glory was coming forth out of the Gates of my heart, going forth as the Warrior King to conquer. He comes out of each of the heart of those who love and honor Him to fulfill all of His purposes. We carry Him within our hearts as He carries us in His. We are naturally ambassadors of Him and His love. Hallelujah!

33 HIS GLORIOUS RETURN

We, the Harvest Fellowship Church at Warrensburg, were worshiping. I had a vision during the 3rd song, "I worship You, O Mighty King, there is none like you!" The worship team brought us into *the Glory*! Our voices were quiet but the music went on beautifully.

A planet appeared to me in a vision. I could see the stars in the background. It was an awesome sight! My thought was *Why would I be seeing a planet?*

Then I saw the Lord Jesus smiling and looking down on a number of them. The planets appeared small compared to Him, about the size of of beach balls. He seemed not a bit surprised that they were appearing before Him. "They are paying homage to Me!" He informed me.

As the first planet spun away, another took its place. Each planet gave its moment of glorifying the Lord. There was a line of planets ready to take their turn. Then the Lord said -"It is time for your planet to come and honor Me!"

It is time for this earth to become completely the Kingdom of our God! And it is going to happen! The sound of the praises of His people will sound from one end of the earth to the other. For there will be no happier people. So grateful we will be that death and sorrow will have passed away. No one will stand, but all of us will bend our knee to the One True Living God, Even Jesus! Hallelujah! Amen and Amen!

One time while I was sleeping I had a dream vision. I looked up and saw the most beautiful sky I had ever seen. Its' blue was azure blue. It was brilliant! There was a group of clouds that formed a bright magenta swirl. Another group glowed with fluorescent orange. All of this was a feast to my artist's eye.

Suddenly, a very small, single black dot appeared in the colorful sky! My curiosity turned into awesome anticipation! The dot gradually expanded so that I could look into heaven, beyond the sky! It had become a portal. It then transitioned into a huge circular opening with angels sitting and standing on the edge of it. Jesus stood above them. The sky and heaven's beauty faded before His awesome beauty!

There was a hush as the angels and all of heaven acknowledged His magnificence! Every one of the angels was looking up at Him breathlessly. I could feel their great anticipation and excitement. Their silent question begged to be answered.

"When is the time for His returning to earth?"

Then I woke up.

Get ready, for He is coming soon!

ABOUT THE AUTHOR

Vivien is a minister, a professional artist, and an author who lives in Missouri, and fervently enjoys her life with God, family, friends and horses.

She has operated in the prophetic and healing ministry for a number of years. Vivien has published a number of Christian books for others as well. She attended, graduated from, and was ordained by Joan Hunter's Healing School located in Texas.

She has given ministry to the Native Americans on the Navajo Reservation at Chinle, Arizona and a short time on the Sioux Reservation in North Dakota. She has a special love for the Native American People.

Her main ministry seems to be encouraging other believers to journey deeper into the Heart of God. She operates in the Supernatural through visions, words of knowledge, and expressing to others God's love and prophetic words for them.

"Knowing Jesus is the most exciting experience anyone can have in this life," states Vivien. "Knowing that He loves us is Life Eternal!"

COMING SOON:

A book based on a vision and word from Father God.

www.ingramcontent.com/pod-product-compliance
Lightning Source LLC
Chambersburg PA
CBHW060739050426
42449CB00008B/1272